Delaware Moor Racial Epitaphs

Delaware Moor Racial Epitaphs

Mixed-Blood Stories Images and Poems

Loren G. Kelly

A Moment in Time Books, LLC

Delaware Moor
Racial Epitaphs

© Loren G. Kelly, 2020

All rights reserved. This book or any portion thereof may not be reproduced or used in any manner whatsoever without the express written permission of the publisher except for the use of brief quotations in a book review.

To request permission, write the author at:
A Moment in Time Books, LLC
1201 Houston Place
Royse City, Texas 75189

or by email:
lorenkellyamomentintimebooks@gmail.com

First Printing

ISBN 9798652597603

Book Design:
Vivian Freeman Chaffin, Yellow Rose Typesetting
Vivian.Freeman@yellowrosetype.com

Printed in the United States of America

Dedication

This work is dedicated to my wise and loving "Delaware Moor" maternal Grandmother, Elnora Parrish Williams, who once told me: "Loren, we all come into this world the same way; upside down and naked. We all go out of this world the same way. In life, titles, fame and money mean absolutely nothing. It is what you do between your birth and death that counts. And Love is the most important thing you will ever do."

Vivian Williams Kelly, my mom; Elnora Parrish Williams, my grandma; Elizabeth Miller Parrish, my great-grandma; and Enoch and Phoebe Carney Miller, my great-great-grandparents, were all descendants of the Delaware Moors, a colonial mixed-race community from Little Creek Hundred, Kent County, Delaware, and existing decades before the American Revolution. These exceptional people, who inter-married with African Blacks (Moors), Caucasians and Nanticoke (the Tidewater people) and Delaware (the Leni Lanape) Native American tribes have maintained a separate and unique community that is older than our nation.

Delaware Moor Racial Epitaphs...Mixed-Blood Stories, Images and Poems is a legacy to my family. This family anthology connects my ancestors across generations in time, to me, my children, grandchildren and all of our future descendants. It is our life story and articulates my love of history, genealogy and poetry. I am here because of those who have gone before me. They are my essence. They are my truth. As I transcribed this family saga, I felt Grandma Williams' presence. Fifty-five years ago, my "Delaware Moor" grandma prophetically predicted that I would become a great scholar and write a book. This is that book.

Loren G. Kelly
AKA: "Pa Pa Kelly"

Also by award-winning author Loren Kelly—

Black Gold, Roughnecks and Oil Town Tales
...as told by a Wildcatter's Grandson

Amazon Kindle Direct Publishing (KDP), 2019

Ageless Authors International Writing Contest, 2020
Nonfiction Category
Finalist—"Oilfield Dad"
Honorable Mention—"Mighty Warriors of Valor"

Silver Leos Writers Guild Anthology, 2020
"Oilfield Dad" (memoir)
"Fortune Telling at Grandma's House" (memoir)
"Evasion" (poem)

Contents

Introduction, 1

Chapter I—Delaware Moor Family History, 11
Seven Generations of My Delaware Moor Maternal Lineage, 12
The Life and Times of Dewitt and Elizabeth Miller Parrish's Children, 15

Chapter II—History of the Delaware Moors, 21

Chapter III—Delaware Moor Tales—Glimpses into Our Past, 27
Grandma's House, 29
Fortune Telling, 36
Family Reunions, 38
Crystal Lake Treasures—Swimming, Fishing and Carousels, 41
Out West—1908, 45
Grandma's Letter—1964, 47
Long Lost Brother, 49
Ma's Precious Secret, 51
Michigan Twister, 53
Delaware Moor Warriors, 55
Thomas Milton Williams: World War II—Battle of the Bulge, 55
Clayton Carlos Williams: World War II—Battle of Buna, New Guinea, 57
Otto Rollin Parrish: World War II—Battle of Hurtgen Forest, 58
Dewitt Larue Parrish: The American Civil War (War Between the States), 60
Private Thomas Carney: The American War of Independence—
Battle of Guilford Courthouse and Siege of Ninety-Six, 62

Chapter IV—Delaware Moor Family Poems, 65
Delaware Moors, 67
Racial Epitaph, 69
A Mother's Secret, 71

Rocking Chair, 73
Roots, 75
Not Forgotten, 77

Chapter V—American Revolution and Civil War Delaware Moor Poems, 79

Freejack Patriot, 81
Freedom, 83
Glory, 85
Slave, 87
Plantation, 89
Slave Ship, 91
Black Moses, 93

Chapter VI—Mixed Blood Poems, 95

Mixed Messages, 97
Labels, 99
Exclusion, 101
Folk, 103
Multi-Racial, 105

Chapter VII—Passing Poems, 107

One Drop, 109
Incognito, 111
Shine On, 113
Belonging, 115
Who We Be, 117
I Never Knew, 119

Epilogue, 121

'Wade in the Water', 123

Acknowledgements, 124

About the Author, 126

Introduction

I am the curator of our family history. Shortly before my mother died, I began researching the maternal side of our family. My mom, Vivian Williams Kelly, abruptly warned me: "Be careful about doing your research; you might not like what you find out." She would not reveal to me what she meant, but I ultimately discovered the family secret, she took to the grave. This book was completed by me out of necessity from a cathartic experience of unearthing our hidden family enigma. Most of my life I understood that I'm White. I look White. I identify as White. Others consider me White. I've been discriminated against for being White–yelled at for being White. My birth certificate says I'm Caucasian. Because I look White, I assumed I was White. Anti-white discrimination affected me and anti-white propaganda insulted me. Imagine this… I woke up one day to discover that I was also Black and Native American. A distant relative advised me of this fact, which I confirmed through genealogy research and DNA testing, using Ancestry.com, in 2004. It was ironical that I had always been *Other*. At fifty-three, it was similar to a mid-life crisis. As a student of history, I stepped up the investigation of my family genealogy, compiling genealogical and historical research over a sixteen-year period. Ultimately, through a journey into my ancestor's distant past, I came to respect who my family really is and that I am part of a remarkable and proud people.

I am just one of millions of people world-wide who have placed a bit of saliva into a DNA kit for testing and discovered a life altering secret in those tiny drops. Virtually every cell in a human's body carries that person's whole unique blueprint—the double helix known as DNA. DNA doesn't lie. It connects us to our ancestors decades and centuries ago. What that means is our ancestors are alive in all of us today. Race is real. It's burned into our DNA. DNA analysis of our genetic code by scientists provides information about our ethnicity and where our ancestors come from. DNA testing contains surprises and raises the question: *Are we really who we think we are?* My DNA, tested through 23andMe DNA, shows I am Black as follows:

- Sub-Saharan African (1.0%)

Further, this one percent of my Black DNA breaks down by specific locations in Africa:
- Nigerian (0.2%)
- Broadly West African (0.2%)
- Southern East African (0.2%)
- Broadly Congolese and Southern East African (0.1%)
- Senegambian and Guinean (0.1%)
- Broadly Sub-Saharan African (0.2%)

Additionally, I discovered my Native American DNA:
- Broadly East Asian and Native American (0.2%)

Another DNA test I took through Ancestry.com indicated that one percent of the blackness within me came from Nigeria. Both DNA tests affected my core identity. I belonged to a different ethnic tribe. I had no cultural knowledge of my African ancestry. The identity that had grounded me and gave me meaning for most of my life had been shaken. Family lore and traditions that had been passed down from generation to generation were now challenged. So I began a search for self by researching my ancestral past.

Following my DNA reveal, my sister and my maternal cousin, both tested their DNA. My sister's results showed that two percent of her DNA is from Nigeria. My cousin's testing showed two percent of her DNA is from Cameroon, Congo, and the Southern Bantu peoples. This further scientifically verified my family's African ethnicity. I have uncovered numerous genealogical documents (Civil War Records, Wills, Land Records, Lists of African American families, and Census Records) in my Family History research that proves my Ancestors were African American. My ancestors fought for the Union during the Civil War, for that very reason.

Further genealogy research by me through The World Tree on Ancestry.com revealed the following:

Dr. Martin Luther King	Ninth Cousin	
Harriet Tubman	Eighth Cousin	Twice Removed
Joe Louis "The Brown Bomber"	Eighth Cousin	Twice Removed
George Washington Carver	Eighth Cousin	Twice Removed
Denzel Washington	Eighth Cousin	Once Removed
Condoleezza Rice	Ninth Cousin	
Jimi Hendrix	Eighth Cousin	Once Removed
Nat King Cole	Eighth Cousin	Once Removed
Michael Jackson	Ninth Cousin	
Whitney Houston	Ninth Cousin	
Otis Redding	Eighth Cousin	Once Removed
Cab Calloway	Ninth Cousin	
Miles Davis	Eighth Cousin	Once Removed
Sammy Davis Jr.	Eighth Cousin	Twice Removed
Sarah Vaughan	Eighth Cousin	Once Removed
Quincy Jones	Ninth Cousin	

These distant relatives are all famous African Americans. Sitting Bull, a Hunkpapa Lakota Holy Man and Indian Chief, responsible for the death of General Armstrong Custer at the Little Big Horn, is my seventh cousin four times removed. Sacagawea, a Lemhi Shoshone woman, who guided the Lewis and Clark expedition, is my fourth cousin four times removed.

When I tell people this story, many do not believe me, because my phenotype (outer appearance) is that of a White man. However, my genotype (DNA) is 1% African and .02 % Native American, scientifically proving that my family on my mother's side is multi-racial. My mother kept this family secret of our Black heritage. She was a Delaware Moor. This meant she had African as well as Native American heritage. In Delaware, my ancestors were part of a closely-intertwined community of families, called the Delaware Moors, who shared a common heritage. The connection was based on race, or the presence of mixed blood: Native

American, White, African American, Moorish, or other origins. Mulatto is the term applied to the Delaware Moors due to their mixed blood. Before and during the Civil War, many people of color in Delaware were not slaves but deemed free. Yet, the "One-Drop Rule" of black blood, classifying anyone with even one ancestor from Africa as Black regardless of skin color, meant those pronounced free by federal law were treated with little to no respect by White Southern society. Persecuted, terrorized, and lynched, they chose to stay closely bonded in their own cultural community for safety sake. Throughout history, Delaware Moors endured the devastation of slavery and perils of race in America. This is my family and their fascinating story.

Although my great-grandmother, Elizabeth Miller Parrish, and her parents, Enoch D. Miller and Phoebe A. Carney Miller were listed by the census taker as free persons of color and mulattos on the Delaware Federal Census, it was not easy for them living under the "one drop" rule. In Delaware, my great-great-grandparents were relegated to a second-class-citizen status of sorts. Federal Law denied Black persons citizenship under the Dred Scott Decision of 1857. "Free-issue," was a term for a free-born Black before the Civil War. This is also probably the origin of "free-jacks," a term used in the late nineteenth century for any free Black person. The attitudes of the "White South" towards "free Blacks," like the Delaware Moors, were the following restrictions on their civil liberties: Freedmen could not hold public office, could not vote, could not testify against a white person, could not bear arms, and had no free assembly. They were subject to curfews. In short, the non-slave Southern Black person was not totally free and he or she did not enjoy the rights of citizenship and the freedoms afforded to other Americans found in the Bill of Rights of the United States Constitution. Even if a Black person could prove their freedom, they enjoyed little higher status than slaves. Discrimination was common against mixed-bloods, like my ancestors. If "slavers" caught freedmen walking around without their "free papers" they would kidnap them and sell them into bondage. Most of the Delaware Moors were land owners, dating from the eighteenth century, before free Blacks were denied the right to own land. As farmers they tilled the land. They weren't sharecroppers or slaves. Delaware was a haven for free Blacks, like the Delaware Moors, at a time when many of their compatriots were still slaves on surrounding farms. Many White residents were envious because some of them were not land owners. That is why the White population in Cheswold, Delaware, were incensed that people of color, like my great-great-grandfather, Enoch D. Miller, could actually own land.

On the 1820 and 1840 Delaware Federal Census for Little Creek Hundred and Duck Creek Hundred, Kent County, Debrix Miller, my great-great-great-grandfather and father of Enoch D. Miller, and his family are listed as *free persons of color* and *Mulatto*. From this same Delaware Moor community, more than a dozen extended families migrated to Michigan in the years 1855-1875. Because of the oppressive laws government passed against *free Blacks,* my maternal great-great-grandparents, fled after 1863, to the North through the free state of Pennsylvania from Little Creek Hundred, Kent County, Delaware, and into the wilderness of Michigan. By escaping from the South, as the Civil War was raging and America was in upheaval, their true race was forgotten. On the 1860 Delaware Federal Census my family had been labeled *Mulatto*. On the 1870 Dallas, Clinton County, Michigan, Federal Census, Enoch, Phoebe and Elizabeth Miller, passed as *White*. Their race was listed as White on every subsequent

Page No. 15

SCHEDULE 1.—Free Inhabitants in Duck Creek Hundred in the County of Kent State of Delaware enumerated by me, on the 8th day of June 1860. Thos Thompson Ass't Marshal.

Post Office Smyrna

Dwelling	Family	Name	Age	Sex	Color	Profession	Real Estate	Personal Estate	Place of Birth	Married	School	Deaf/etc
		George S. Bason	2	M					Delaware			
		Joseph L.	1/12	M								
		George Warren	24	M		Farm Hand						
		Samuel Jones	10	M	B							
89	88	Mary Jones	30	F	B					X		
		Lydia	8	F	B							
		Amanda	2	F	B							
90	89	Isaac Sutton	29	M		Farmer		752	New Jersey			
		Mary A.	25	F					Penna			
		James Haggard	20	M	B	Farm hand			Del.			
		James McCartney	13	M					Penna			
91	90	Alexander Duty	27	M		Farmer		672	Del.			
		Mary J.	20	F								
		Helen A.	1/2	F								
		James Jones	17	M	B	Farm hand						
		George Duff	10	M	B							
		Nicholas Durham	58	M	M	Farm hand						
92	91	Henry Durham	50	M	M	Laborer						1
		Rachel	30	F	M							1
		Enoch	6	M	M							
		Maria	4	F	M							
		Agnes H.	1/2	M	M							
93	92	Enoch Miller	43	M	M	Farmer		350				1
		Phoebe	36	F	M							1
		Dettick	17	M	M							
		Thomas	13	M	M							
		Elizabeth	11	F	M							
		Enoch	9	M	M							
		Morris	7	M	M							
		Augustus	5	M	M							
		Eliza	1/2	F	M							
94	93	Philip Clayton	23	M	M	Laborer		35				
		Anna	22	F	B							

1860 U.S. Census taken at Duck Creek Hundred, Kent County, Delaware, listing Enoch and Phoebe Miller and family as Mulatto.

Page No. 3

SCHEDULE 1.—Inhabitants in the Township of Dallas, in the County of Clinton, State of Michigan, enumerated by me on the 6th day of July, 1870.

Post Office: Dallas

F. Byron Carter, Ass't Marshal.

431

#	Dwelling	Family	Name	Age	Sex	Color	Profession, Occupation, or Trade	Real Estate	Personal Estate	Place of Birth	11	12	13	14	15	16	17	18	19	20
1			Elzada	40	F	W	Keeping House			New York										
2			Lewis	15	M	W	Farming & at school			Michigan						/				
3			Harriet	12	F	W	Attending school			New York						/				
4			Eugene	10	M	W				Wisconsin						/				
5	19	18	Trombly Ferdinand	38	M	W	Carpenter			Canada East	/	/							/	
6			Martha	19	F	W	Keeping House			New York										
7			Eliza	16	F	W	At Home			Michigan	/	/								
8			Mary	14	F	W				Michigan	/	/								
9			Joseph	13	M	W	Works on Home Farm			Michigan	/	/								
10			Louisa	11	F	W	Attending school			Michigan	/	/				/				
11	20	19	Nickerson Hiram	35	M	W	Farmer	1500	610	Michigan									/	
12			Mary	36	F	W	Keeping House			England	/									
13			Charles	13	M	W	Attending school			Canada West					/	/				
14			George	10	M	W	"			Michigan	/				/	/				
15			John	8	M	W				Michigan	/									
16			Aurelia	6	F	W				Michigan	/									
17			Emma	2	F	W				Michigan	/									
18	21	20	Harris Allen	45	M	W	Farm Laborer	100		New York	/								/	
19			Eliza	35	F	W	Keeping House			New Jersey						/				
20			Elmer	4	M	W				Michigan										
21	22	21	Brooker Frederick	58	M	W	Farmer	900	465	Mecklenburg, Ger.	/	/							/	
22			Fredericka	34	F	W	Keeping House			Mecklenburg	/	/								
23			Alvina	11	F	W	At School			Michigan	/	/				/				
24			Anna	8	F	W				Michigan						/				
25			Frances	6	F	W				Michigan						/				
26	23	22	Cuddeback George	32	M	W	Farmer	3300	3350	Pennsylvania									/	
27			Elizabeth	26	F	W	Keeping House			Indiana										
28			Elnora	7	F	W				Illinois						/				
29			Arthur B.	5	M	W				Michigan										
30			Oscar	2	M	W				Michigan										
31	24	23	Timmons Absolom	25	M	W	Farm Laborer		130	Pennsylvania									/	
32			Emily	24	F	W	Keeping House			N. York						/				
33			Mosher Leota	12	F	W	At Home			Michigan						/				
34	25	24	Miller Enoch	50	M	W	Farmer	1600	530	Pennsylvania						/	/		/	
35			Phebe	47	F	W	Keeping House			Pennsylvania						/	/			
36			Morris	17	M	W	Works on Home Farm			Pennsylvania										
37			Augustus	16	M	W	"			Pennsylvania										
38			Eliza	10	F	W	Attending school			Pennsylvania						/	/			
39			Rebecca	8	F	W				Pennsylvania						/				
40			Ellen F.	3	F	W				Michigan										

1870 U.S. Census taken at Dallas Township, Clinton County, Michigan, listing Enoch and Phoebe Miller and family as White.

Federal Census, because my family was light complexioned enough to pass as White. They had successfully integrated into White society by fleeing to the North. Passing as White afforded my family the opportunity to be citizens of these United States. Before passing, we had no rights in our own country. Passing meant we were free.

Unknown to the surrounding White ruling class, for one-hundred and fifty years, from 1870 to 2020, my maternal lineage secretly passed as White. The human being has a history of being awfully cruel to someone who is different. If you were different, people would talk down to you, talk around you, or look down on you. As free Black folk in the antebellum South my family was different, but we were truly sons and daughters of America, deserved of respect. Our family, once a veiled mystery obscured in darkness, is now illuminated by this memoir to the world. The reality is going back four to seven generations, before the 1870 Census, my Delaware Moor ancestors were considered to be of African (Black) descent. On the 1870 Michigan Federal Census and every Census thereafter my family has passed as White. Inevitably what changed was Enoch D. Miller's and Phoebe Carney Miller's, as well as their descendants, desire to be totally free by masquerading as White people.

Enoch D. Miller's, my great-great-grandfather's, Delaware Civil War Draft Registration Record, dated July 1, 1863, listed his race as colored. According to the 1860 Delaware Federal Census, my maternal great-grandmother, Elizabeth Miller, and her entire family's race were listed as "M" in the race column—an abbreviation for Mulatto. Mulatto was an old nineteenth

U.S. Civil War registry listing Enoch Miller, my great-great-grandpa, as a colored man.

century term intended to mean a person of mixed European (White) and African (Black) descent. Further research revealed that my Miller and Carney ancestors are listed as free African Americans in *Free African Americans of Maryland and Delaware, from the Colonial Period to 1810,* published by Clearfield.

Introduction: This is the history of the free African American communities of Maryland and Delaware during the colonial period as told through their family histories...

Miller Family: **Jacob Miller,** *born say 1705, was taxable in Little Creek Hundred, Kent County, Delaware, in 1727, taxable in Murderkill Hundred from 1735 to 1738 when he was identified as a "Negro," and taxable in Dover Hundred from 1756 to 1765. He sued Tabitha Francisco in kent County in August 1731 (RG 3815.031, Common Pleas, Dockets 1722-1732, Frame 509). He was called Jacob Miller (Negro) in Kent County court when John Holiday sued him for debt in November 1737 and on 26 February 1747 when he admitted in court that he owed Robert Willcocks 27 pounds (RG 3815.031, Common Pleas, Dockets 1733-1740, frames 347, 358; 1744-50, 388) He may have been the ancestor of...*

> *viii.* **Deberox,** *born 1776-1794, head of a Duck Creek Hundred, Kent County, household of 7 free colored in 1820 (DE:49). He left a 5 April 1841 Duck Creek Hundred, Kent County, will, proved 22 April 1841, naming his wife Sarah, children Josiah, Elijah, Enoch, Robert, and Rachel; and grandchildren Rachel and John Hews, children of his daughter Maria (WB R: 197)....*

Excerpt from: *Free African Americans of Maryland and Delaware From the Colonial Period to 1810*
—Paul Heinegg (May 17, 2018 [2000])

In the late nineteenth century, there were about three hundred families of this diverse race called the Delaware Moors, living in and around the small town settlement of Cheswold, Delaware, in the heart of Kent County, located sixty-eight miles from Philadelphia Pennsylvania. In 1856, as a depot stop along the Delaware Railroad, Cheswold, Delaware, was first called Leipsic Station. Then in 1860 it was renamed Moorton after John S. Moor, who owned a General Store and most of the land in and around the town. Finally, in 1888 a contest was initiated to rename Moorton. The new name for Moorton became Chesswold; composed of *chess* which came from a large group of Chestnut trees near the train depot and *wold* which means forest or trees. It was later shortened to Cheswold. My Delaware Moor ancestors lived in the surrounding countryside and community, since before 1776. Being different, my family intermarried within the Delaware Moors, because they did not believe in marrying outside of their culture. Because of this, they were isolated from the rest of society and kept to themselves.

At a distance, a Delaware Moor looked like any ordinary Black person living in this tiny community. They had their own Methodist church, a school, and a number of houses scattered around a central avenue. Closer scrutiny revealed they were not totally Black. Some of them were so fair and light complexioned they were often mistaken for White persons.

African Americans have been part of our American story since the very beginning. In 1619 some of the first enslaved Africans arrived in Jamestown, Virginia. Although some would gain their freedom and own land, like the Delaware Moors, most remained as slaves. Over the next two-hundred-plus years slavery became a key part of America's economy, particularly in the South. By 1861 there were about three to four million slaves. Slavery created a social memory of when human beings were treated as things or property, instead of as people.

The Thirteenth Amendment to the Constitution officially abolished slavery in the United States and was adopted on December 18, 1865. The Civil War officially ended in April of 1866. Reconstruction began and although slaves were supposed to be freed, segregation took hold in the South. Segregation required separate housing, education and other services for people of color.

Segregation was made law several times in eigthteenth and nineteenth-century America, as the South believed Black and White people were incapable of living together. Legal segregation in public facilities was current from the late nineteenth century into the 1950s, because of the Jim Crow Laws of the South. Slavery officially ended in 1865, but lived on in a different form as states passed anti-miscegenation laws barring interracial marriage. This became the justification for Jim Crow segregation laws that followed. Shockingly, Mississippi failed to ratify the Thirteenth Amendment to the Constitution, ending slavery, until one-hundred and forty-eighty years later in 2013.

Twentieth-century America saw a long struggle of equality for Blacks. This racial justice battle was fought to put right the wrongs of slavery and segregation. One-hundred years after the Civil War, the Civil Rights movement of the 1960s sought equal rights for Blacks, who still did not have the same status as Whites. The Civil Rights Act was finally passed in 1964. Those that went before, as enslaved human beings, deserved to have their progeny live as a free people. It wasn't until *Loving vs. Virginia* (1967), a case involving a White man and Black woman, that the U.S. Supreme Court declared state laws prohibiting interracial marriage unconstitutional. It was this history of racial discrimination and laws against interracial marriage, or miscegenation, which caused my mother to live in fear of someone discovering she was part Black, until the day she died. Texas, where my parents lived from the 1940s, had an active Klu Klux Klan who beat and murdered Blacks on a regular basis. It is sad to me that my mom had to pass as White and lived in fear of her and my dad being jailed, beaten, tortured or murdered by lynching, simply because they were in an interracial marriage. Given the racial injustice of those turbulent times, I totally understand her fears that if our ancestral secret were to be revealed, it would be at great peril to our family.

Over time my mixed-blood family dynasty has faded. Enoch D. Miller died in Montcalm County, Michigan, on October 14, 1893, at the age of seventy-three. He is reportedly buried in the Carson City Cemetery, located in Carson City, Montcalm County, Michigan. His widow, Phoebe A. "Libby" Carney Miller Richardson (she remarried a John H. Richardson), died on

March 14, 1911, at age eighty-seven and is buried in Home Township Cemetery in Edmore, Montcalm County, Michigan. My Great-Grandmother Elizabeth Miller Parrish was born on November 25, 1849, to Enoch D. Miller and Phoebe A. Carney Miller in Duck Creek Hundred, Kent County, Delaware. She married Dewitt Larue Parrish, settling in Stanton, Montcalm County, Michigan, and died there on July 2, 1937. Great-Grandmother Elizabeth Miller Parrish is buried in Forest Hill Cemetery in Stanton, Michigan. My maternal Grandmother (Elnora Parrish Williams) was the daughter of Elizabeth Miller Parrish, My mother was born July 28, 1916, in Stanton, Michigan. When I was growing up, Stanton, Michigan, was where I would visit my Delaware Moor Grandma Elnora Parrish Williams, every summer, until her death in 1968. My mother, Vivian Williams Kelly Honea, died on March 3, 1990, leaving me, my siblings and cousins as the last vestiges of our Delaware Moor family. Some would say that by passing for over four generations my family is Black no more. But by writing this book I have exposed, hidden deep within our Delaware Moor genes, the souls of our Black folk bloodline.

As the African American poet, Maya Angelou, once said: "History despite its wrenching pain, cannot be unlived. But if faced with courage, need not be lived again." Up until the last part of the twentieth century, multi-racial people did not have the opportunity to choose identities for themselves. Today a person of mixed ancestry, like myself, can choose to embrace all parts of his or her races. We can learn a lot about race from the Delaware Moor experience. Being a Delaware Moor was positive, in that it provided a source of belonging, mutual help, and self-esteem within that population.

Identified as a group of mixed-bloods who shared a sense of identity, a common history, and mutual experiences, Delaware Moors are free persons of color, with varying proportions of White, Native American, and Black blood. Due to their particular racial mixtures, this group has been historically recognized as lower socio-economic status, sharing their family units with neither Whites, Blacks, nor Native Americans. They survived racial animus by isolating themselves from and eventually blending into American society. They have been called The Yellow People—a distinct group of several hundred families who intermarried. For over three-hundred years their culture has maintained a separate and unique community, despite all attempts to force assimilation by the White man. I am proud to be descended from this remarkable people and consider it an honor to call them my ancestors.

Sisters—Carrie Parrish Bennett, Elnora Parrish Williams and Emma Parrish Miller in front of the Williams house in Stanton, Michigan, 1939.

CHAPTER I

Delaware Moor Family History

Seven Generations of My Delaware Moor Maternal Lineage

Thomas Carney Jr. (1758-1828) and **Mary Harris Carney** (ca. 1750)
Great-Great-Great-Great-Grandparents—Direct Ancestors (seven generations)
During the American Revolution, he was a free man of color who enlisted in the Fifth Maryland Regiment in the spring of 1777, serving for three years, and carried a wounded Captain Perry Benson off the battlefield during the Battle of Ninety-Six in South Carolina in June 1781 [National Archives pension file 535203 cited by NSDAR, *African American Patriots,* 181 (M 804, roll 473, frame 552, https://www.fold3.com]. He was head of a Duck Creek Hundred, Kent County, household of four "other free" in 1800 [DE:24] and a "negro" head of a Caroline County, Maryland, household of seven "other free" in 1810 [MD:190]. Also listed in *Free African Americans of Maryland and Delaware from the Colonial Period to 1810* by Paul Heinegg (2018).
Married on 14 May 1771 in New Castle County, Delaware.
Children: Thomas N. Carney

Thomas N. Carney (1776-1856) and **Sarah Hewes/Hughes** (1810-1860)
Great-Great-Great-Grandparents—Direct Ancestors (six generations)
Children: Rebecca Carney, Levi Carney, Gustavus Gustavern Carney, Morris Carney, Cornelia Ann Carney, Sarah Sally Carney, Eliza Carney, and **Phoebe A. Carney** (Miller)

Jacob Miller (1705-ca. 1765) and Unknown Wife
Great-Great-Great-Great-Grandparents—Direct Ancestors (seven generations)
Children: Aaron Miller, Rake/Rike/Right Miller, **Deberox/Debrix Miller,** John Miller, Isaac Miller, Peter Miller, Haste Miller, and Charles Miller

---

Debrix/Deborix/Deberox Miller (1781-1841) and Sarah Ann Counselor/Concilor (1787-1850)

Great-Great-Great-Grandparents—Direct Ancestors (six generations)
Children: John Hughes Miller, Rachel Miller, Maria(h) Miller, Josiah Miller, Elijah Miller, Redmond Raymond Miller, **Enoch D. Miller,** and Robert Miller

---

Enoch D. Miller, Sr. (1820-1893) and Phoebe A. Carney Miller (1823-1911)

Great-Great-Grandparents—Direct Ancestors (five generations)
His Parents: Debrix/Deborix Miller and Sarah Ann Conselor/Concilor Miller
Her Parents: Thomas N. Carney and Sarah Hewes/Hughes Carney
Their Children: Debricks Miller, Charles Miller, Thomas Miller, Enoch Miller, Morris M. Miller, Augustus Miller, Eliza Ann Miller, Rebecca Miller, Ellen Frances Ella Miller, and **Elizabeth L. Miller**

Elizabeth L. Miller Parrish (1849-1937) and Dewitt Larue Parrish (1844-1913)

Great-Grandparents—Direct Ancestor (four generations)
Her Parents: Enoch D. Miller Sr. and Phoebe A. Carney Miller
Her Siblings: Debricks Miller, Charles Miller, Thomas Miller, Enoch Miller, Morris M. Miller, Augustus Miller, Eliza Ann Miller, Rebecca Miller, and Ellen Frances Ella Miller.
His Parents: Asa Parrish and Mary Ann Coykendall Parrish
His Siblings: Arvilla, Catherine, John C., Mary E., Charles Asa, William Roy, Mary Elizabeth, and Ellen Francis.
Their Children: Seymour D., Arthur, Carrie E., Emma, Lettie Dell, Maude Ella, and **Elnora Parrish**

Elnora Parrish Williams (1881-1968) and Lewis Milton Williams (1874-1960)

Grandparents—Direct Ancestors (three generations)
Her Parents: Dewitt Larue Parrish and Elizabeth L. Miller Parrish
Siblings: Seymour D., Arthur "Archie," Carrie E., Emma, Lettie Dell and Maude Ella.
His Parents: Edwin P. Williams and Amy Gay
Their Children: Ruth Avalyn, Lester Roland, Clayton Carlos, Thomas Milton, and **Vivian Madeline Williams**

Vivian Madeline Williams Kelly Honea (1916-1990) and Luther James Kelly (1907-1972)

Parents—Direct Ancestors (second generation)
Her Parents: Louis Milton Williams and Elnora Parrish Williams
Her Siblings: Ruth Avalyn, Lester Roland, Clayton Carlos and Thomas Milton
Husbands: Ralph E. Williams, Luther James Kelly, and William Odes Honea
Her Children with Ralph Williams: John Warren Morse (Adopted)
Luther Kelly's Parents: Nathan Tompkins Kelly and Laura Rebecca Kelly Stateler Williams*Luther Kelly's Siblings:* Hugh David, Laura Maitlen, Nathan Tompkins Jr., Carl S., Doratha Rebecca.
Vivian and Luther Kelly's Children: Richard James, Lanora Ellen, and **Loren Gerald Kelly**

Loren Gerald Kelly (1951-   ) and Barbara Juanita Sickler Kelly (1958-   )

Son—first generation
His Parents: Luther James Kelly and Vivian Madeline Williams Kelly
His Siblings: Richard James and Lanora Ellen.
Her Parents: Edward Calvary Sickler and Alice Juanita Quinn Sickler
Her Siblings: Nelson, Tom Calvary, David Edward, and Mary Ellen.
Their Children: Shaun Brian Ruoff (Deceased), Michael Jeremy, James Ryan, and Rachel Anne

Loren Kelly, age seven, in his Texas cowboy hat as Grandpa Lewis Williams looks on from his doorway in Stanton, Michigan, (1958).

The Life and Times of Dewitt and Elizabeth Miller Parrish's Children

Maude Ella Parrish Kunz (1887-1930)

Maude Ella Parrish Kunz, the youngest daughter of Elizabeth Miller Parrish and Dewitt Larue Parrish, was born on June 2, 1887, in Michigan. She was my mother's, (Vivian Williams Kelly) favorite Aunt. Aunt Maude was a beautiful woman with hair so long it touched the floor. She brushed it over a hundred strokes each night. Maude married Lorenz Eckardt Kunz on February 15, 1916, in Manhattan, New York. She was twenty-nine and he was twenty-seven. Lorenz was from a wealthy family and was employed by the Jamestown Lounge Company in Jamestown, New York. He was a prominent furniture salesman in Grand Rapids, Michigan, before moving to Albuquerque, New Mexico, due to illness. Lorenz and Maude were married only two years when he passed away on February 15, 1918. Maude was at his bedside in their Albuquerque apartment.

Maude returned to Michigan where she was part of Grand Rapids "High Society." She had no children and treated Mother like her only daughter, taking her on cruises and buying her nice clothes. Mom told me that she and Aunt Maude were very close. Maude died in my mother's arms on June 22, 1930, of a ruptured gall bladder. She was forty-three and my mother was thirteen. Maude and Lorenz are not buried next to each other.

Lettie Dell Parrish Scoby (1883-1966)

Lettie Dell Parrish was born on December 7, 1883, in Michigan. She married Joel Van Scoby in 1907 in Kent County, Michigan. They lived in Grand Rapids with their two sons, Dudley (b. January 2, 1916), and Herman (b. February 19, 1916). Her husband, Joel, was short and heavy-set. He had a bad heart and was on disability in his later years. She and Joel were church-going people.

Both sons served in the United States Army during World War II. Herman was wounded when he stepped on a pill box. After the war Herman suffered from Shell Shock and was in constant pain. Today we refer to it as Post Traumatic Stress Disorder (PTSD). In an attempt to self-medicate, Herman drank himself to the point of death, because at that time nothing

was done for GI's returning home from the war. Mom told me, she and cousin Herman were close and he used to take her to dances at Crystal, Michigan. Herman D. Scoby passed on November 21, 1948, in Grand Rapids, Michigan, at the young age of thirty-two and was buried in Tallmadge, Michigan. His brother, Dudley E. Scoby, died on May 5, 2002, in Dade City, Florida, at the age of ninety-two. He was buried in Irons, Michigan.

I remember Great-Aunt Lettie kept her gray hair cut short and only wore gray dresses with white collars. Considered to be a very thrifty woman, she rented out an upstairs bedroom. The exterior of her house was painted gray with red trim. The interior walls were also gray and a spiral staircase with a mahogany banister led to the second floor. Drapes in the house were so dark purple they were almost black and were always drawn closed to keep out the light. She had overstuffed, bright red sofas and chairs, and her kitchen table was gray with red trim.

Great-Aunt Lettie always had a pretty yellow, singing canary in a gold cage. It would chirp and trill incessantly. When one canary died she would bury it and buy another one. She loved the chirping sound of her canary. Her heavy pancake make-up was so thick you could scrape it off with a knife and she always wore bright red lipstick. Lettie was a friendly jovial person and a hugger. She hugged visitors upon arriving and as many as twenty times before leaving. She left a lot of lipstick on my cheek when she bent over to kiss me. I also remember red rouge against powdery cheeks. Relatives were always welcome at Lettie's house in Grand Rapids, Michigan. Great Aunt Lettie died on April 15, 1966, in Grand Rapids, Michigan.

Elnora Parrish Williams (1881-1968)

Elnora Parrish was born on September 29, 1881, in Crystal, Michigan, and married Lewis Williams on November 23, 1901, in Stanton, Montcalm County, Michigan. They had five children in twenty-one years: Ruth Avalyn Williams Nichols Chorman Pratt born August 24, 1902, in Lansing, Michigan; passed June 1982 in Boynton Beach, Florida, at the age of seventy-nine. Lester Roland Leroy Williams, born October 5, 1910, in Lansing, Michigan; passed on December 19, 1996, at eighty-six years; buried in La Crosse, Wisconsin. Vivian Madeline Williams Kelly Honea (my mother) born July 28, 1916, in Stanton, Michigan; passed on March 3, 1990 in Mesquite, Texas, at seventy-three years; buried in Borger, Texas. Clayton Carlos Williams born July 8, 1921, in Stanton, Michigan; passed November 3, 1999, in Gowen, Michigan, at seventy-eight; buried in Greenville, Michigan. Thomas Milton Williams born May 24, 1924, in Stanton, Michigan; passed on October 16, 1991, in Carson City, Michigan, at sixty-seven; buried in Stanton, Michigan.

Elnora also gave birth to two stillborn girls. One was named Ellen and whose name was given to my sister, Lanora Ellen Kelly Owens.

Grandma Williams' hair turned white in her older years and she washed it with Fels-Naptha Laundry Bar Soap to keep it from turning yellow. As a young woman, grandma wore her long hair pinned up in a bun, but cut it shorter as she got older. A favorite past time was crossword puzzles and she was very good at them, keeping us amazed by knowing words unfamiliar to her family. We looked forward to Grandma's Christmas box each year wrapped in brown paper and tied in brown twine. It usually contained a couple of oranges, horehound candy, old-fashioned ribbon candy, packages of Beeman's and Black Jack chewing gum, hazel nuts, walnuts, brazil nuts, pecans (all in the shell), hard candy with a flower in the center as well as hard soft filled candy.

My sister, Lanora, remembers sitting on the bed with Grandma and trying on all the jewelry she kept in a basket. Grandma also sent Lanora, a floral handkerchief for every holiday. She had quite the collection of ladies handkerchiefs by the time she graduated high school. Grandma Williams upheld a tradition of the nineteenth century and earlier twentieth centuries by giving Lanora a red autograph book. She signed it: "Compliments from Grandma Elnora Williams," and also added the following classic poem:

Dear Lanora:
Were mine the power,
I'd twine for thee,
A crown of Jewels rare,
Each gem should be a kingdom
Each pearl, a humble prayer.
—Elnora Parrish Williams
Stanton, Michigan
November 4, 1956

Elnora Williams also wrote the following in Mother's, Vivian Williams Kelly Honea's, memory book:

Dear Vivian:
When the nights are dark and dreary
 and you no more I see.
Remember it was mother that
 wrote these lines for thee.
—Nora Williams, mother
September 1, 1931

Elnora died on January 4, 1968, in Stanton, Michigan, at the age of eighty-six. That winter the ground was too frozen to dig a grave and they had to wait until spring to bury Grandma Williams.

Emma Parrish Miller (1874-1950)

Emma Parrish Miller was born on June 19, 1874, in Clinton, Michigan. She married George Edward Miller in 1899. Their only child, Karl George Miller, was born on March 3, 1903. Karl was a classically trained violinist and concert pianist. He passed on December 18, 1976, in Laguna Hills, California, at the age of seventy-three, and was buried in Lake Forest, California. Em was a very classy lady. She was always very thin and dressed like she had just walked out of a fashion glamour magazine. She was wealthy. Aunt Em was never arrogant nor conceited about having a lot of money, and monetarily helped her family. Em often gave her sister, Elnora, money and took her on shopping sprees.

She was an elegant lady who wore diamond rings and nice dresses. Great-Aunt Emma was intelligent and knew a lot about the stock market. She associated with "high society" people and Em smoked long slender cigarettes. In the 1930s she also drove a brand new car which was highly unusual during the Great Depression. She was considered an independent woman for her time. Em used the nickname "Skinner" for her husband. George was an alderman of the first ward in Stanton, Michigan, and a prominent shipper of potatoes. He was also Stanton fire chief for several terms. George died in 1933 at the age of fifty-eight. Emma died on July 23, 1950, in Lansing, Michigan, at the age of seventy-six, and was buried in Stanton, Michigan.

Carrie E. Parrish Bennett (1873-1944)

Carrie E. Parrish Bennett was born on January 19, 1873, in Clinton, Michigan. She married Romain M. Bennett on April 8, 1893, in Stanton, Michigan. They had two children during their marriage.

Her daughter Ruth Ivy Bennett was born on March 30, 1894, in Stanton, Michigan, and passed away on February 1, 1895, when she was less than a year old. Her second daughter, Iva

May Bennett was born on September 29, 1895, in Stanton, Michigan, and passed away on April 4, 1897, when she was one year old. Carrie died on January 28, 1944, in Stanton, Michigan, at the age of seventy-one and was buried there.

Affectionately known as Aunt Cad, Carrie lived in the largest and oldest two-story house in Stanton, Michigan. Prominently built on a hill, the house was beautiful with shiny woodwork throughout the interior and huge columns on the front porch. Cad kept her house spotlessly clean all of the time. The aroma of freshly baked cookies and cakes often drifted from her kitchen. Cad was a thin little lady who wore her hair up in a bun and a long white apron over her dress. She had dark olive skin and spoke in a low crackling voice.

Her husband, whom she called "Romey," could be a mean man, at times, but was careful how he acted around Cad, because she took a broom after him. As Romey Bennett lay dying, he called his brother-in-law Lew Williams to his bedside. He told Grandpa Williams, "Lewis change your ways! I saw the Devil! I'm going to Hell! It's awful there!" Romey then began screaming and pleading with the doctors not to let him die. His was a hard death. Grandma Williams said it was such an awful sight to see him die as a raving maniac. Great Aunt Cad died a few years later.

Obituary for Carrie E. Parrish Bennett

Services Held Sunday for Carrie E. Bennett—Funeral services were held at eleven o'clock Sunday morning from the Stebbins and Co. Funeral Home here for Mrs. Carrie E. Bennett, who died at the home of her sister, Mrs. Lew Williams here Friday evening following a brief illness. Born January 19, 1873, at Fowler, in Clinton County, she had spent over sixty years in this community, with the exception of a few years in Idaho and Lansing. She was married to Romaine Bennett at Stanton in 1893. He preceded her in death December 14, 1943. She was a member of the Vickeryville Protective Association. She is survived by three sisters, Mrs. Elnora Willams of Stanton, Mrs. Emma Miller of Lansing, and Mrs. Lettie Scoby of Grand Rapids; and a brother, Seymour Parrish, of Lansing. Rev. Clyde Lee of Stanton officiated at the service and interment was made in Forest Hill Cemetery.

Arthur "Archie" Parrish (1869-1944)

Arthur "Archie" Parrish was born on July 30, 1869, in Oakland, Michigan. He married Phoebe Ann Baddis Parrish on December 22, 1898, in Stanton, Michigan. They had five children in twelve years. Loyd D. Parrish was born on November 23, 1899, in Stanton, Michigan; passed on May 9, 1968 in Lansing, Michigan, at sixty-eight; buried in Stanton, Michigan.

Orval Parrish was born in March 1901 in Michigan; passed at six, on May 17, 1907, in Michigan. Mildred L. Parrish was born on August 19, 1904; passed on April 1978 at seventy-three; buried in Okemos, Michigan. Donald Dean Parrish was born on February 19, 1906 in Michigan; passed on January 13, 1971, in Lansing, Michigan, at sixty-four. Otto Rollin Parrish was born on April 23, 1912, in Lansing, Michigan; passed on October 5, 1945, in Liege, Belgium, at thirty-three; buried at the Ardennes American Cemetery in Neuville-en-Condroz, Liege, Belgium, due to being killed from a mortar shell. Arthur Parrish died on January 4, 1944, in Lansing, Michigan, at seventy-four; buried in Stanton, Michigan.

Seymour Parrish (1868-1956)

Seymour Parrish was born on March 26, 1868, in Canton, Michigan. He married Myrtle (Myrtie) Daisy Newman Parrish on April 8, 1893, in Stanton, Michigan. They had seven children in fifteen years. Raymond Dwight Dewayne Parrish, born on July 5, 1897, in Stanton, Michigan; passed on May 9, 1971, in Andalusia, Alabama, at seventy-three. Another son, Raymond D. Parrish, born in 1898 in Michigan. Arthur Adison Parrish, born on July 9, 1899, in Lansing, Michigan; passed on February 23, 1953, in Macomb, Michigan, at fifty-three. Howard Marion Parrish, born on April 5, 1903, in Stanton, Michigan; passed on July 20, 1996, in Lansing, Michigan, at ninety-three; buried in DeWitt, Michigan. Ruth E. Parrish, born on February 2, 1908, in Lansing, Michigan; passed on August 28, 1965, in Byron, Michigan, at fifty-seven. Norma M. Parrish, born on May 5, 1910, in Michigan; passed on July 15, 1952, at forty-two. Myrtle Louise Parrish, born on August 9, 1912, in Michigan. Seymour died on October 14, 1956, in Lansing, Michigan, at eighty-eight.

Seymour was a man about town and all of the ladies thought he looked like the actor Maurice Chevalier with his walking cane and straw hat. Women loved him. He was a great dancer and was gifted at sweet talking women. Never driving a car, he walked everywhere. Seymour played piano by ear and kept a grand piano downstairs in his house on Ottawa Avenue in Lansing. He and son Raymond often teamed up for piano duets. Even though he was her Grandma's brother, cousin Shirley called him Grandpa, because she and her parents, Lester and Norine Williams, lived with him in Lansing during World War II, while her father worked at the Oldsmobile plant. He used to bounce my cousin Shirley on his knee. Uncle Seymour was a very loving and intelligent renaissance man.

CHAPTER II

History of the Delaware Moors

Because I am the storyteller of my tribe, I began a quest to reveal my Delaware Moor history. It evolved into my passion, and developed from an immense hunger and thirst to learn everything that I could, and ultimately fostered this book. This amazing story of my ancestors was long lost and forgotten, until I had the audacity to dig it up. Genealogists, like myself, shake the family tree. We then dig up the bones of our family and reassemble the skeleton. The mixed-blood Delaware Moors have been a part of this country's fabric for centuries. In today's discourse about race, multiracial people, like me, are often characterized as if they're raceless. I am White, and I am NOT White, too. I am also African American and I am Native American, and none of these races necessarily exclude the other. Mixed-race people are all of their races. A common occurrence in our society is that many mixed people are not allowed to self-identify as multiracial. Denying people the right to identify themselves as multiracial is detrimental to them. I have disclosed to people my ethnic identity only to have others deny it, saying something like, "That's not possible, you don't look Black," as if the other person is an expert on the way mixed-race persons are "supposed" to look. This happens often because my phenotype is that of a White man, but my DNA includes African and Native American genes. I am truly of mixed-blood, but throughout the years I have experienced invalidation of my racial identity over and over again by people who are unwilling to accept that I am tri-racial. These types of comments can make multiracial people feel as if they are not "the norm," or are different, simply because the person making the comment may not recognize or know of many mixed-race people. This disbelief and denial by others of who I really am affected me so much that I began to show people my DNA ethnic breakdown through Ancestry.com on my cell phone. I have proven Black genes are present inside me, through DNA testing. By looking at pictures of my ancestors faces over time I can see the ethnicity of African and Native American features in them. This same African and Native American ethnicity is also within me. When I mention that I am a Delaware Moor, many people have a confused look and advise me that they have never heard of them. So I begin to explain my ancestral Delaware Moor story.

Delaware Moors were recognized as an unmistakable ethnic group many centuries ago. They settled in nearby Little Creek Hundred, Delaware, about 1710, where they owned and farmed more than a thousand acres of land between them, and until the early twentieth century, maintained their own schools and churches. During World War I and World War II they insisted on being listed as a separate race, lobbying Congress for the distinction, but were denied. In the 1950s the State of Delaware allowed them to place an "M" for Moor on their driver's licenses as a concession to the race request. Delaware Moors had particular facial characteristics that set them apart from both Whites and Blacks. The darkest had brown skins and the lightest resembled their white neighbors. Some of these mixed bloods are distinctly Native American in appearance. Among the immediate families, siblings could look Black, White or Native American. Light skinned parents often had dark skinned children and dark skinned parents often bore light skinned children.

Distinguishable from the overall population, many of my ancestors were concentrated in lowland areas of Delaware along the tidewater of the Atlantic, where swamps, islands or peninsulas offered protection from the outside world. In the eighteenth century, the Moors of Cheswold originally lived in a marshy area along the Delaware Bay settling further inland to farm in and around Cheswold, Kent County, Delaware, during the latter part of the nineteenth century. The children and grandchildren of these families frequently married within their community. It was customary for Moors to marry Moors, extending bloodlines throughout the area. Because of this, Delaware Moors consisted of members of closely interrelated families of racially mixed hybrids.

Ethnonyms are names used to refer to an *ethnic* group, tribe, or people. Some of the folkloric, legendary, and traditional ethnonyms used to label my ancestral Delaware Moors are: mulattos, free persons of color, yellow-people, freedmen, Triracial Isolates, freejacks, mixed-bloods, mystery-people, racial-islands, marginal peoples, submerged races, afro-amerindians and melungeons; which probably derives from French méglanger, meaning to mix.

Delaware Moors are an ethnic group referred to as a "remnant" community. They claim lineage in three different ethnicities: Caucasian European, African, and Native American. They survived in Cheswold, Kent County, Delaware. To escape the racist tendencies of others near their community, they kept their ancestry to themselves, intermarried with neighbors and blended into White society. Over the decades, their outward appearance became less distinctive as a specific ethnic group. In other words, today they look no different than most other people of Caucasian descent. But, they share a common history with Native Americans and African Americans. Legally, inhabitants of these communities were considered non-White, regardless of the color of their skin. Census, government, tax, and church records reveal they were lumped together and labeled as "mulatto." If the ethnicity of those being counted was not obvious to a census taker, they were mulatto. A mix of racial contradiction; they met and mingled. Delaware Moors lived "cheek by jowl," as a rub between White and Black. They challenged cultural norms of the times. Once stereotyped as "free Blacks," they were destined to live a life of racism and exclusion in the South.

My Delaware Moor ancestors shared an unusual history and their origins span back in time over three-hundred years ago, before America was birthed as a nation. Like other common folk, they helped to build this country. Without them there would be no America. Their voices cry out from our nation's past on the pages within this book. Sinning by drinking, dancing, and playing music on Saturday nights. Purifying themselves in Church by praying and singing gospel music on Sunday mornings. Fighting for freedom in America's wars; though very often denied their own freedom. They lived and loved in the shadows; stirring the American melting pot. After the Revolutionary War, the racial climate in Delaware changed drastically. Mixed blood people who had appeared in the official records with no racial classification suddenly became "mulattos," "free colored people," even "negro." Regarding the Delaware Moors, early White settlers labeled these racial intermediates free Colored or "free Negroes" and considered them as mere squatters rather than as legitimate settlers on the land. The laws were interpreted to the disadvantage of these folk and they were forbidden to testify in court. Acts were passed to prohibit their movement to/from other states and they were considered undesirables since they bridged the racial gap between free Whites and slave Negroes. After the Civil War these mixed folk were still classified as colored or as mulattos, but they were frequently encouraged to develop their own institutions and schools. Delaware Moors were ostracized by Blacks, and Native Americans as well as Whites.

One popular legend tells of these Delaware Moors being descended from a captive Moorish sailor—who turned out to be a Prince of the Congo—sold as a dark-skinned Moroccan slave to a beautiful wealthy Irish woman, called Requa, who bought him and bore his mixed-race children. Shunned by the White community, they moved inland and joined Nanticoke Indians. Eventually the blood of Moors (Africans), Whites and Nanticoke Indians blended and the combination of these three races spawned the tri-racial Delaware Moor of today. Gradually Nanticoke Indians, once numerous in Southern Delaware, disappeared, but many of their descendants are now the Delaware Moors.

Many of the Moors were almost pure white in color, while some were yellow, and others a deep brown. Other residents in and around Cheswold, observing these fair-faced Delaware Moors, labeled them the "yaller" (yellow) men or mulattos. The "One-Drop Rule" in the American South was a social and legal principle of racial classification which asserted if any person had even "one drop" of Black blood (African ancestry) they were legally Black.

On October 8, 1855 State Attorney General, George P. Fisher, prosecuted Delaware Moor Levin Sockum for selling shot and gunpowder to a "Negro or mulatto," his future son-in-law, Isaac Isaiah Harmon, also Delaware Moor from Sussex County. At that time, there was a law forbidding anyone from selling or loaning ammunition to a Black man or a mulatto. The legal action was brought by a group of White men who had a grudge against Sockum. Harmon claimed he was Indian and therefore exempt from this law. When Harmon appeared in court, everyone was surprised, expecting that he would be of "yaller" (yellow) or Black blood. Instead, Harmon's complexion appeared to be almost that of a White man. He had chesnut hair and hazel eyes. Harmon had been described by the prosecution as Black or mulatto. It was apparent to the jurors that Harmon was of a race that was altogether different. It was important for the prosecution to determine if the legal claim was true; that Harmon was Black or mulatto, and therefore that Sockum was guilty of a crime. So Fisher's star witness, an eighty-seven- year-old woman considered the last Nanticoke to speak the language of the tribe and a relative of Harmon named Lydia Clark was called to the witness stand. She proceeded to prove in the eyes of the court that Harmon's ancestors were in fact part Black. Lydia told the story of the origin of the Delaware Moors as described above. She testified the original forbears of the Delaware Moors appeared about twenty years before the American Revolution and the succeeding generations were mixed blood Blacks, Whites, and Indians. The jury believed her testimony. Sockum's verdict was guilty in the Sussex County court, because Lydia Clark had established to the jury the Delaware Moors were not totally Indian (Nanticoke) or White, but were of Black (African) blood as well. Sockum was convicted, fined $20 and made to pay the court's costs. The trial outcome was that Levin Sockum was at least part Nanticoke, probably with White and/or Black blood, making him "colored" in the eyes of his White neighbors.

For people living in bondage, Delaware in the 1820s through the 1860s, was a land of antebellum plantations and hot dirt floor wooden slave quarters where a slave's family tree ended in a bill of sale. Slaves were owned by another person like a chair, a horse, or a piece of property. Children were sold away from their mothers and wives were sold away from their husbands. Slaves were forced to do their master's bidding, no matter how cruel the demand. A slave's disobedience resulted in violent punishment, torture, and sometimes death. Even worse, the abuse was sanctioned by Southern society. Slaves were considered inhuman by their White masters. They picked the cotton, plowed the tobacco fields, cooked the food and helped raise their owner's children. Slaves knew they were human beings, but were forced to endure horrific servitude, suffering, and deprivation that denied their humanity. They were aware their life was not their own. Race is the concept of dividing people into populations or groups on the basis of physical characteristics resulting from genetic ancestry. Slavery placed racial labels on dominated people and created negative myths regarding people of color, making it easier for the dominators to ignore the humanity of their victims.

Racial dominance made it easier for Slave owners to rationalize holding their fellow humans in bondage, whipping them, selling them, separating their families, and working them to death. Multi-racial groups like the Delaware Moors threatened this system of racial domination. Delaware Moors were "free people of color," but not slaves past the 1720s. What kept them out of the loop of African American history was that they had White and or Native American ethnicity in their maternal line. Colonial government in the mid-colonial period determined "race' and social standing using the mother's racial listing. In other words, you were what your mother was. This is also true in most Native American cultures. Because they were part Nanticoke Indian, the Delaware Moors went into hiding in and around the swamps of Delaware to avoid being moved onto reservations as other tribes were.

In 1850 the United States Census Bureau came out with the racial categories of "B" for black and "M" for mulatto. Mulatto is defined as a person with one Black and one White parent and became a term for anyone who could not be racially categorized, including Native Americans. The term mulatto was applied to the Delaware Moors, because they were not just one race. Most historians and cultural anthropologists called the Moors of Delaware "tri-racial isolates," because they were socially isolated and married only within their group of people.

Because it was a border state, slavery was not outlawed in Delaware during the Civil War. The northern part of Delaware was above the "Mason Dixon Line" and Kent County, where my ancestors lived, was south of the "Mason Dixon Line," making it a part of "Dixie." Free Blacks, like my ancestors, held themselves to be above slaves in social status. However, they were still looked down upon by Whites living in Kent County. Delaware Moors were considered a threat to the Southern way of life and were persecuted by White Southerners. Most White slave owners regarded free Blacks as dangerous; a living denial of slavery and a bad influence on their slaves. Southern Whites feared free Blacks might encourage slave revolts and began to reign in their freedom before and during the Civil War. In 1832 the Delaware General Assembly passed "Black Codes" to control the lives of freedmen. "Slavers" would kidnap free persons of color and sell them into slavery. Soon these harsh rules made Delaware the worst place in the Union for freedmen prior to the Civil War. Laws were passed limiting emigration from state to state. The result was an exodus of Delaware free Blacks northward during and after the 1850s, including my maternal great-great-grandparents: Enoch D. and Phoebe Carney Miller and their daughter Elizabeth Miller.

1952 Williams family reunion on the front lawn of Aunt Avalyn's farmhouse in Sparta Michigan: Lewis Williams, Elnora Williams, Mary Jean Chorman, Vivian Williams Kelly holding author Loren Kelly, Lanora Kelly, Avalyn Williams Pratt, Tom Williams, Richard Kelly, and Luther James Kelly.

CHAPTER III

Delaware Moor Tales: Glimpses Into Our Past

Grandma Williams' home with the winding dirt road leading to her house. Our Shasta travel trailer and 1963 Chevy Pickup are parked in front (ca. 1967-1968).

Grandma's House

Every summer, during the 1940s, 1950s and 1960s, Mom, Dad, and three kids would travel the Interstates and state highways of America with our small Shasta sixteen-foot travel trailer hitched behind our Buick Special or Chevrolet Pickup, on a road trip from Phillips, Texas, to Stanton, Michigan. Our mission was to visit my Delaware Moor Grandma, Elnora Parrish Williams, and Grandpa Lewis Williams. Once we arrived in Mom's, hometown of Stanton, Michigan, we drove down the long dusty lane to Grandma Williams' house. Walking up to the front door we would knock to enter. Grandma greeted us at the door and gave my mom and all of us kids big hugs and lots of kisses. She was always glad to see us. As we walked through the welcoming front door of Grandma's house, we hung up coats, hats, umbrellas as necessary in the entryway. My mother remembered sub-zero winter days when she opened the front door to find a wall of snow blocking the way. A shovel was kept inside the entryway to dig their way out.

Using a skeleton key, we opened the door leading from the entryway into the dining room. The first things we saw were the dining table and chairs staged directly in front of us. Grandma's kitchen was to the left with an old iron stove where she cooked fantastic meals. She had all kinds of hanging plants adorning the kitchen and others placed artistically throughout the house—rubber plants, Christmas cactus, spider cactus with long hanging vines, aromatic smelling lavender, beautiful lily blooms and wild violets planted in vintage jardinière pots. Grandma loved plants and flowers of all kinds. One of her long forgotten gardening tips was to poke a rusted railroad spike or rusted nails into the dirt surrounding potted plants, because the rust helped the plants to grow. Grandma definitely had a green thumb.

In her kitchen, Grandma Williams pulled out her iron spider from the pantry and placed it on top of her behemoth stove top. Grandma's spider pan (a nineteenth-century invention) was a large iron frying pan, with legs protruding from the hammered base and a rat-tail handle. The thick iron worked as a flattop griddle. Cooking with lard right out of the can, Grandma fried up big sugar cookies inside this iron spider. Then she planted a currant in the middle of each warm cookie, pressed it down with her wrinkled thumb, and richly sprinkled the entire cookie with sugar. They were so good, that we immediately asked for another. She also made huge molasses cookies that melted in your mouth in this same iron spider. Not having the money for expensive ingredients, Grandma found ways to take her modest cooking to the next level, like pouring dry cherry Jello powder and a dash of coffee into a cheap boxed chocolate cake mix to make a decadent cherry chocolate cake. Her innovative cooking methods made her pies, cakes, and cookies taste like expensive desserts.

Strained bacon grease was Grandma's secret to making the best fried potatoes—mixed with onions—and the most delicious and flaky pie crust. Her mashed potatoes were the best I ever ate. Grandma always sat down while peeling potatoes. She placed these peeled potatoes in a big kitchen kettle and cooked them for hours. After draining, she mixed lard and butter coloring—which came in a one-pound box—into the potatoes along with condensed milk. Grandma then used an old wooden masher, beating the potatoes with a frenzy until she created fluffy mouth-watering mashed potatoes. These scrumptious mashed potatoes were spread over white bread for us to eat. Grandma and Grandpa Williams were poor folks and often times did not have meat for their meals.

When they did have meat, it was furnished by Aunt Avalyn who brought a live chicken from her farm in Sparta, Michigan. Grandma wrung the chicken's neck, cut off its head and feet, then dipped the whole bird in paraffin wax, plucking out the feathers, after the paraffin dried. The chicken was then cut into pieces, which were dipped in an egg wash and rolled in cornmeal, then fried in the iron spider. I remember the aroma and biting into the crunchy skin as grease dribbled down my chin. The taste was wondrous. Homemade biscuits, mashed potatoes, and fresh peas were hearty sides for this bountiful meal fit for a Queen or a King. Grandma Williams loved to make hot green tea enjoyed by my mom. She placed the loose tea leaves in a china cup on a saucer with a matching flower design. Grandma boiled the water on the stove and when it was ready, poured the boiling water over the loose tea and covered the cup with the saucer, allowing the tea to steep for several minutes to enhance the flavor. She added mint leaves and sometimes milk, but no sugar.

A huge white rectangular sink sat right beside the stove. Grandma handwashed her dishes and rinsed them in the deep sink. On the right side were grooves, where she placed the dishes, so the water drained back into the sink. Grandma always told my sister, Lanora, to sit down while washing dishes, so she wouldn't get so tired. In fact, Grandma did most of her housework while seated, regardless of whether she was washing dishes, peeling potatoes, folding clothes or ironing. Clothes were pressed using old flat irons that were alternately heated on the stove. The irons had to be held with potholders due to the intense heat. Her ironing board was made of wood and covered with a white cloth—that had turned brown from the hot flat irons.

Grandma Williams slept in the bedroom just past the kitchen. To keep ne'er-do-wells from breaking into her house, she kept several wooden bats under her bed. One day, Grandma grabbed one of her bats from under her bed, showed it to me, shook it menacingly, grinned a wicked grin, and said, "Nobody better try to harm me in my house, I will beat them to a pulp!" I was reassured she would protect me against all evil doers. Bats weren't the only things Grandma hid in her bedroom. She kept money, rolled up in her nylon stockings and for some reason, hid giant conch seashells from Lake Michigan under her bed. One of the conch sea shells had a hole in it, and if you blew into it just right, echoed throughout her house. Grandma enjoyed demonstrating this to me when I was a little boy.

She had an old iron bed frame that was painted enamel white with an old mattress that sunk in the middle. The worn pillows were hard with feathers stuffed inside the fabric that stuck us through the pillow case. All of us kids wanted to sleep with our grandma. Grandma tucked my sister, Lanora, into bed at night on the edge of the mattress, because the center sank in so much. The bed was covered in homemade heavy patchwork quilts tucked around us, keeping us from moving around. We were wrapped up like little mummies. All the grandkids were allowed to sleep until noon and when we woke up we with feathers in our hair from the pillows.

Grandpa's bedroom was on the other side of the dining room, across from Grandma's. They had separate bedrooms, because they were always yelling at each other and arguing. For many years, Grandpa Lewis Williams was night watchmen for the City of Stanton, Michigan. My Aunt Winnie Hallock Williams told me that as kids they would sneak up on him in the early morning hours, giggling and staring at him as he snored and slept in his small guard shack. He was usually tired from a long night of playing cards and drinking while on the job. Grandpa's drinking continued to an extent that in his later years, he began to experience symptoms of dementia. Grandpa Williams also became a junk man who visited the local dump, taking my cousin Shirley with him, when she was a little girl. Lewis Williams fixed and sold the stuff that he found at the dump.

The scariest place for us kids inside Grandma Williams' house was the cellar that lay beyond a door in her bedroom. When I was a kid I would grab a large pink mint candy from Grandma's candy jar to boost my courage, then slowly open the squeaky door. Spiders and cobwebs got into my hair as I fearfully creeped down the creaky handmade wooden stairs into the earthen cellar. I could see about four inches of blue sky through a small window on the right side as I inched down the cellar steps. Shelves higher than your head contained glass Mason jars. This dimly lit menagerie of jars held pressure cooked fruits like apples, peaches, cherries, and berries, as well as jams, jellies, and various vegetables. Their contents resembled the remains of dead monsters. All of the canned goods were displayed in a neat row, lining the shelves in front of the window. With Sunlight from the small window as the only illumination, I had to retrieve these goods from the cellar depths during the daytime when there was natural light. The cellar's dirt walls and floors were always damp and musty smelling. It reminded me of a rotting grave. The grandkids usually avoided the cellar, like it was the plague.

As scary as the cellar was, the upstairs to grandma's house was just as mysterious. A door in the wall just off the dining room gave people access to the upstairs. As a child, I was never allowed to go up there, but my cousin Shirley was more adventuresome and liked to sneak upstairs to play. Grandma used to get on to he, saying it was considered too dangerous for a little girl to explore. One day, Shirley found her dad's knickers from his childhood and wore them home. Her father, Lester teased her mercilessly—accusing her of trying to dress like a boy. Grandma got pretty mad, scolding her son for the transgression of making his daughter—one of her favorite granddaughters—cry. There were plenty of old hats, dresses and other clothes for Shirley to play dress up in, keeping her entertained for hours on end. Dusty steamer trunks, oil lamps, boxes of old books and the remains of a wooden rocking chair and an antique iron bed also occupied the upstairs space, along with Great-Grandfather Dewitt Parrish's fiddle and his Civil War cavalry sword and spurs.

Beyond the kitchen and dining room, the living room housed a white wicker chair, couch, and a huge homemade wooden rocking chair that all of us kids rocked in. We were always afraid we would rock over the tail of Grandma's black and white dog, Rex. Other furniture consisted of odds and ends from the 1930s and everything was painted white. Hand-embroidered cloth doilies were delicately placed on some of the furniture.

Large French doors, painted white and embedded with glass panes, led into the parlor, which also served as the music room. A huge, old fashioned, upright player piano with rolls of music set along one wall. Accompanied by Uncle Tom on the violin, my grandma sat on the rotating stool in front of this piano which we could also play like a regular piano with the entire family gathered around on Friday or Saturday nights singing songs and hymns. Grandma, Uncle Tom, Uncle Lester, Aunt Avalyn and my mom all played the piano by ear.

The parlor held additional wicker furniture, including a huge table where grandma practiced her gift of second sight by reading tea leaves. An antique mahogany Victrola phonograph with a huge metal flower-like speaker was positioned on a stand in the corner. Someone had to wind the handle several times in order to rotate a turntable, before placing the stylus in the grooves of thick dusty records. The music emitted from this record player had a scratchy tinny sound.

A Dutch half-door connected the parlor to a long six-foot wide room, which ran the entire length of the side of the house. Grandma stored chests, outdoor games, bicycles, and other sundry items in this room Cousin Nancy and I used as a playroom. We played board games, told ghost stories, and attempted to predict our futures. The planchette of a "Ouija Board" eerily moved, as we lightly placed our fingers on top, producing cryptic messages. As we asked questions of this "talking board," the top half of the Dutch door slammed shut, scaring us. It was as if the "spirit board" was warning us of things to come.

An exterior door led from the playroom into a field where we caught fireflies in Mason jars. Holes were poked in the lids, providing an air supply for the insects. hen we used the jars like lanterns to light our way at night. Playing with neighborhood kids was always fun. We cut small saplings from the field adding a piece of string for bows and arrows. Or cut giant rhubarb leaves the size of elephant ears and placed them over our heads like umbrellas when it rained. A dump existed by the house where people tossed their worn out junk. Cousin Nancy always worried we might disappear into the dump's abyss when Dad backed up our travel trailer close to the edge. One of the few vivid memories I have of Grandpa Williams is him grabbing me with his rugged old-man carpenter hands, saving me from tumbling down the hill into this perilous trash dump.

Going to the bathroom at Grandma's was quite the adventure. Her house was not plumbed for an indoor bathroom, instead we made restroom trips to the outhouse. To get to the small shed we walked through the front door, turned to the right past the apple orchard, continued down the hill toward the railroad tracks, and behind Grandma's house. Our safety conscious grandma always told my sister to be careful when she visited the outdoor toilet, because gypsies and hobos hung around the railroad track area and would kidnap her. She was also advised to be on the lookout for bears, because a bear had drug a neighborhood baby into the woods and ate it. We also had to watch for snakes slithering in and around the outdoor latrine. This necessary place was a tall, skinny, wood shack with a half-moon cut out of the front door, allowing light to enter. If it wasn't for the moon shining at night or the sun shining during the day, we would not be able to see inside the dark privy. The only lock was a hook and eye latch, similar to an old-fashioned screen door, meant to keep out bears, hobos and gypsies. Inside a rough flat wooden board extended the width of the shed with a round hole cut in the middle. Grandpa Williams sanded this rough board to prevent splinters from sticking into our bare behinds. A heavy piece of wire attached to the inside wall held the toilet paper roll. If the toilet paper ran out, carefully placed inside the outhouse was a *Sears Roebuck Catalog,* as a substitute. The outhouse always emitted quite the stench. Uncle Lester was born inside this outdoor toilet during Grandma Williams' trip to the restroom. She had to retrieve her baby from the bottom of the outhouse. Grandma always said Uncle Lester was born premature, weighing just one pound, and that he could fit inside of a shoebox as a newborn.

We loved playing in the orchard. One day as my six-year-old sister, Lanora, was playing between the apple orchard and the house when she saw a snake. She was scared and hollered, "Snake!" Grandpa Williams heard her scream and ran out of the house, grabbed a hoe, and chopped off the snake's head with one whack! The trees in the apple orchard were also easy to climb, and as a little girl, Lanora climbed up an apple tree, following our older brother, Richard. Richard climbed out of the tree, but wouldn't help her down. So Lanora screamed in terror and Grandma Williams ran out of the house, climbed the tree, and helped her granddaughter. Quite a feat for an elderly lady in her sixties. Grandma loved her grandkids very much. Cousin Shirley Williams also liked to climb grandma's apple tree and eat the green apples, although they always made her sick. All of us grandkids enjoyed climbing and carving our initials and hearts with "who loved whom" in the tree bark.

During a neighborhood yard day sale, Grandma Williams came into possession of a group of baby chickens. Lanora, Richard, and Shirley kept pestering her to give them each a baby chick. Finally, Grandma told them they could have one when she died. For weeks, they approached Grandma and asked how she was feeling. Grandma wasn't happy and no one ever got a baby chick. Eventually, the chicks grew into hens and ended up on Grandma's dinner table.

On another day Mom and Grandma ran through the house screaming, because a bird had flown through an open door. Grandma grabbed a broom and was swinging it wildly at the bird, trying to get it out of her house. Afterwards, my superstitious Grandma Williams told me a bird flying inside a house was a sign that someone was going to die.

Grandma always wore velvet gloves, a pillbox ribbon hat, and was usually all dressed up with a purse dangling from her arm whenever she went anywhere. Aunt Avalyn, dressed just like Grandma, would pick her up after church on Sundays and take her to eat at Brownies Restaurant in downtown Stanton, Michigan. Mother and daughter enjoyed a nice meal and finished it off with pie and coffee. My grandma was a Christian woman and attended the First Congregational Church in Stanton, Michigan. That congregation met in a huge Victorian house. Later the building was occupied by Trinity Bible Church.

Every Sunday all of Grandma's kids and grandkids gathered at her house for supper and to play cards. Inevitably the card playing turned into a fight. Grandpa Williams would say, "I've got three hooks!" To which Grandma Williams replied, "What's three hooks?" "Three Jacks!" Grandpa answered. Grandma would get mad and exclaim, "Lew Williams, you're cheating!" And the fighting commenced. Cousin Shirley's dad, Lester Williams, would get into an argument with Aunt Avalyn, slamming his fist through the middle of the card table, sending money and cards flying everywhere. Lester ripped up the card table and tossed it into the ravine behind the house. Aunt Avalyn angrily proclaimed she was never playing cards again, but she always came back and things started all over again the next week. At times the fighting got so loud the townspeople heard them all the way downtown. People would ask, "What is all that noise and racket!" Then someone would say, "Oh that's just the Williams playing cards." The hardware store downtown kept a supply of card tables, knowing my Uncle Lester would be in on Saturday to buy a new one for Sunday. While the dishes were washed and the food put away after supper and before the card playing began, the family enjoyed singing. Uncle Tom played piano and Aunt Avalyn sang. The problem was that Avalyn had a singing voice that sounded like a screech owl. Everyone cringed when Aunt Avalyn tried to hit those high notes. Cousins Suzanne and Shirley, as well as the rest of the family, gathered around the piano, singing loudly in a futile attempt to drown out Avalyn's high-pitched harsh voice.

A favorite activity at night was sitting outside in Grandma's front yard and looking up at the night sky. In the 1950s we warily observed the Russian Sputnik traveling overhead. We were constantly alarmed the Russians might attack us from outer space. Grandma pointed out the Milky Way Galaxy, which appeared as a milky band of light in the dark night sky, the North Star, Big Dipper, Little Dipper, Orion the Hunter and the Seven Sisters—the seven stars from the Pleiades star cluster. Grandma taught us about the Man in the Moon and the Rabbit in the Moon. Grandma also told us kids God would never permit man to land on the moon. On especially dark Michigan nights we could sometimes see the Aurora Borealis, also called the Northern Lights. These shimmering curtains of green to purple light shows blazed across the night skies. We watched the lights curve, curl, slither and flicker. The lights danced and darted here and there. It was unbelievable. We squealed at the breathtaking heavenly light show across the canvas of a Michigan night sky. Such was life at my Delaware Moor Grandma's house.

Grandma and Grandpa Williams were married on November 23, 1901. Grandma was anti-alcohol and Grandpa loved to drink. Not a match made in heaven, but they were married for fifty-nine years. One day while Grandma had guests in the parlor, Grandpa Williams—in the latter stages of dementia—ran into the room naked, wielding a butcher knife, and chased the ladies around the house screaming and stabbing in the air. Previously he had burned the neighbor's apple orchard. Grandma became afraid of Grandpa and she and Uncle Tom had him placed in an insane asylum in Traverse City, Michigan, for his and everyone's protection. I remember Grandpa Williams, as a quiet man and I always thought he looked like Abraham Lincoln. Grandpa died in 1960 in this insane asylum. I was only nine years old.

After my Grandma passed in 1968, the house was emptied and over time fell into disrepair and eventually the ceiling caved in. Uninhabitable, the house was condemned and torn down by the city. The dusty lane to what was Grandma's house is now covered by grass. The railroad tracks behind her house, where hobos used to ride the rails and gypsies camped out in the 1930s and '40s are no longer in use. Many of Grandma's Delaware Moor family are buried in the local Forest Hill Cemetery.

Most of my relatives are now long gone—lost treasures of another time. A few of us grandkids remain. And I am now a grandpa. Only my special memories and a few curiosities from Grandma's house survived throughout these many years. I still have Grandma's rotating piano stool, her antique Delaware rocking chair, and the big conch sea shell that she used to blow like a horn. As a tradition, I blow the conch shell every New Year's Eve at midnight. Such family heirlooms are a reminder of this great lady and our Delaware Moor family, whom I loved dearly.

Cousins Mark Forsberg and Nancy Williams in a field across from the front yard of Grandma Williams' house in Stanton Michigan, about 1966.

Fortune Telling

My Delaware Moor grandmother, Elnora Parrish Williams, was born with a veil over her face, meaning her face was covered born with an unbroken amniotic membrane (veil) at birth. Medical journals call it being "born with the caul" or Caput galeatum (helmeted head) in Latin. Those born with the caul or "caulbearers" have been scientifically observed as possessing gifts of clairvoyance and other types of "supernatural" abilities and are extremely intuitive or gifted. Psychic research also supports these observations. In Grandma Elnora Williams' case, it was believed that she was psychic and could see into the future by reading tea leaves.

My psychic Grandma Elnora Williams, in the 1930s, as she helped local police find a missing body.

To begin the session, Grandma and her guest sat at her parlor table where Grandma placed loose green tea leaves in a broken handled tea cup. She poured warm water over the tea leaves from a china teapot and together the two gently tipped the cup allowing water to spill slowly into the saucer. The tilted cup was rotated in a single direction until all of the water was emptied out of the cup and left in the saucer. In order to get a more accurate reading of the person's future, she advised her guest not to shake the cup. Grandma then held the cup up to the light, looking intently at the glistening tea leaves remaining on the walls and bottom of the cup. She was able to read the symbols in the tea leaves and interpreted the meaning of the tea leaves as they applied to the person whose fortune was being told. The tea leaves were her way of channeling her psychic ability. Grandma turned the tea cup for my Dad's future and after looking at his tea leaves, she became startled and refused to tell him what she saw. I believe she foresaw the pain and suffering from the cancer that would take his life.

Mom and Dad had to agree before Grandma read their children's fortunes. Grandma told Lanora she would have great responsibility taking care of a lot of people and she saw her all dressed in white. She further advised Lanora would be working with women dressed in black with white around their faces. The first time Lanora worked as a nurse's aide was at St. Mary's Catholic Hospital in McAlester, Oklahoma. The nuns were dressed in black tunic habits with headpieces and a black veil in the back that covered a coif of white outlining their faces. Grandma also told Lanora she saw her dressed in all white with a hat perched on her head giving her even greater responsibility. After eleven years as a nurse's aide, Lanora passed her state boards as a nurse, scoring the third highest in her class. At graduation she received the stripe on her nurse's hat and officially became a Licensed Practical Nurse.

My cousin Shirley visited Grandma's house and had her fortune told. Grandma Williams advised Shirley it would be a long time before she found happiness. Cousin Shirley had two failed marriages before she married for a third time and was much happier. Grandma also advised Shirley she would inherit some money, which she did.

Learning of my grandma's psychic abilities, ladies from the community came to her house to have their fortunes read. Even though Grandma refused to charge a fee for her fortune telling, these ladies dropped money on her parlor table before they left. Many came back to my grandma and said their fortunes had come true. In 1966, when I was fourteen, Grandma Williams read my fortune in the tea leaves. She told me I was dressed in a blue uniform and surrounded by many men in khaki colored uniforms. She also stated I was surrounded by violence, death and destruction, and the chaos was enclosed by green walls. According to my grandma, I was safe, while others around me were seriously hurt. I assumed this meant serving in the military during the Vietnam War.

In 1980 I worked as a Federal Correctional Officer, dressed in a blue uniform, and surrounded by inmates wearing khaki uniforms. A prison riot broke out and inmates were destroying furniture and tables as well as beating and stabbing each other with handmade shanks. I was in full riot gear and protected from the inmate rampage. As I looked around me I saw the green walls of the El Reno Federal Correctional Institution. At that very moment I experienced a flashback to Grandma Williams' fortune telling and instantly recognized this was the situation she had predicted fourteen years earlier.

Grandma Williams felt it was wrong to charge money for her gift. My mother and sister related a story to me about a wealthy woman dressed in furs and jewels, who came to Grandma's parlor. As she was reading her fortune, grandma advised this woman not to go into a dark place, because someone would do her harm. The woman laughed, mocked Grandma, threw money in her face, and left. Not long afterwards, this woman wandered into a dark wooded area where a man came out from behind a tree and hit her in the head with a rock, killing her. Police detectives interviewed my grandmother about this woman's death. She told them what she had seen in the tea leaves and where they could locate her body. Grandma Williams' story was written in a true crime magazine about helping the police locate this woman's dead body. The event occurred in the 1930s, long before psychics became well-known for assisting the police in finding missing and murdered people.

Grandma Elnora Williams and me in front of her house in 1967, a year after she told my fortune

Family Reunions

Avalyn Williams Pratt, Grandma Williams' daughter, lived on a farm in a two-hundred-year-old farmhouse, outside of Sparta, Michigan. This short lady was a fantastic cook proved by her over three-hundred pounds. Williams' family reunions were held at her farm during the summer. Avalyn became the matriarch and glue that held our family unit together. As kids we sat in a huge white four-person yard glider swing suspended between two huge black and white bark birch trees in the front yard of her farmhouse. We also climbed and played in those old trees. As Aunt Avalyn prepared the food for the family reunion, our mothers chatted about family and observed us through a huge picture window, while the men discussed the price of gas, farming, and politics in the sitting room.

The adults ate at the dining room table, which seated about twenty people. When the weather was good, the adults sat at picnic tables in the backyard. The children were relegated to the kids' table, located just off the dining room in an enclosed porch or at a folding table by the backyard picnic tables. Kids had to sit at a separate table, because we were prone to dropping food and spilling stuff. We were not allowed to sit at the adult table until we graduated from high

My family at Aunt Avalyn's farm, breaking bread during a family reunion.

school. Taking your place at the adult table was a rite of passage in our family reunions. It was a big deal when you could look back and smile at younger, envious siblings and cousins still seated at the Kiddie Table.

A white linen table cloth covered the adult dining room table set with fine china plates, porcelain cups and saucers, polished silver utensils wrapped in linen napkins and lead crystal goblets. The outside adult picnic tables and kids' tables contained paper plates, plastic cups and plastic eating utensils. The adults consumed tea and coffee, while the children drank Kool-Aide or cold unpasteurized milk. I especially liked the fresh cold water pumped from the farm's well pump with its delicious mineral taste.

If you entered Aunt Avalyn's house you had better come prepared to eat. If you didn't eat, she wanted to know what was wrong with you. To Avlayn food and eating represented love and family. She prepared multitudes of farm to table food and placed it on the buffet serving table. Heaping hot platters of sliced roast beef, turkey, ham, fried and baked chicken were followed by big bowls of steaming hot mashed potatoes, dressing, brown gravy, green beans, corn, cheeses, salads, relishes and other tasty sides.

These sumptuous dishes were accompanied by homemade bread and rolls with freshly churned butter. And don't forget the wide selection of desserts with platters of fudge, cookies, chocolate cake, and lemon meringue, cherry, apple, chocolate, and coconut cream pies. She made sure you ate more than one piece of pie. Plus, she always had an Angel Food Cake topped with strawberries and fresh whipped cream and several varieties of flavored Jello molds. It was a smorgasbord of food the likes of which I have not seen since.

After partaking of this huge amount of food it was time for the outdoor games. I remember setting

At our family reunion, about 1952, on the front lawn of Aunt Avalyn's farm house. (Left-Right) Grandpa Lewis Williams, Aunt Avalyn Pratt, Grandma Elnora Williams, Sister Lanora Ellen Kelly, Mary Jean Chorman (cousin Eddie's wife), Vivian Madeline Kelly (Mom) holding me (Loren G. Kelly), brother Richard James Kelly, Uncle Tom Williams, an unknown farm hand, Cy Pratt and Aunt Avalyn's Dog, Whitey.

up the grass playing field for croquet. Using croquet mallets, we placed the wire hoops (wickets) at strategic places around the yard and pounded the wooden goal stakes into the ground at either end. We smacked our striped wooden balls with mallets across the field of play attempting to knock our opponent's ball out of play while getting our own ball to the goal stick for a win. Since we were a competitive bunch, this normally subdued game became quite lively. My uncles erected a badminton net where we batted the shuttlecocks with our racquets back and forth over the net. The shuttle cocks flew everywhere. When we tired of badminton we used this same net for volleyball. And when playing volleyball with my cousins and family…let's just say it was game on.

Softballs and bats were always available and everyone wanted to hit that special homerun. We cousins also flew kites and ran and played with Whitey, Aunt Avalyn's white spaniel-mix farm dog in the recently harvested cornfields. Cousins Nancy and Suzanne Williams, Mark Forsberg, and me liked to sneak into the big red barn full of rectangular bales of hay. The hay was held together with bailing wire and stacked real high. The perfect playground for us. We tunneled through the loose hay and climbed onto the stacked bales and jumped into the blanket of hay below. We played fort, pirates, cowboys and Indians in the hay barn. It was quite the escapade.

Uncle Larry and Aunt Avalyn survived on what they raised on their working farm. They had an orchard with apple, peach, and cherry trees. They filled bushel baskets with fruit for public sale. Strawberries, blackberries, blueberries and raspberries were placed into quart containers and sold to people passing by their farm as well as at local stores.

Larry tilled a huge plot of land with his tractor every spring and planted corn, lettuce, green beans, and onions. Aunt Avalyn stayed busy all summer canning fruits and vegetables. They also grew superior flowers like tulips, roses, carnations, and peonies for local flower shops as well as townspeople who understood the price savings.

When visiting I was tasked with pouring the liquid slop into the trough for a hog the size of a Volkswagen and several pigs, a unique experience for me. My Aunt and Uncle milked several cows and the milk produced tasted very good.

All of us kids enjoyed gathering the eggs, but only after we got over our fear of the mother hens. We wore rubber booties over our shoes to protect them from chicken poop and carefully entered the chicken coup. Avalyn gave each of us a metal pail and told us to take the eggs from beneath the mother hen, but she invariably pecked our hands. Feeling sorry for us, Aunt Avalyn showed us how to move the hens to the side. The old mother hens flapped their wings and ruffled their tail feathers as they flew into the air. Uncle Larry and Aunt Avalyn sold lots of eggs, and the extra income helped pay for vacations. The farm was such a lucrative business that they took many trips in their travel trailer to Florida and Arizona, as "snowbirds," avoiding the harsh Michigan winters.

Crystal Lake:
Swimming, Fishing and Carousels

Near Stanton, Michigan, located in the northeastern part of Montcalm County, is Crystal Lake. This lake sparkles like a crystal as its pretty waters reflect the sunlight similar to a mirror. Originally named Silver Lake this pretty body of water is fed from springs distributed around the lake bed. The lake's sandy bottom is outstanding for swimming and you can wade a great distance before reaching a depth greater than six feet. The lake is fairly shallow, but about three-fourths of a mile from the resort area is the deepest portion at seventy feet. The lake's waters are clear and its shores rise to considerable heights, covered with oak and pine. The southeast and northeast shores offer cozy cottages providing the comforts of a summer resort. Whether driving or walking, you'll cover eight miles to travel the shoreline. Boaters cover one and a half miles if going from end to end.

Grandpa Williams, a carpenter and bridge builder, built many of the cottages from stones removed from the lake. Picnickers and excursionists enjoy a small island accessible from the shore and near Crystal Township located on the southeast shore of the eight-hundred-acre body of water. Crystal was founded on April 1, 1868, and people frequently visited this village during the warm summer months to enjoy the pleasures of Crystal Lake. My family often visited Crystal Lake for summer recreation.

Luther Kelly, my father, loaded his green tackle box full of fishing line, hooks, multi-color painted wooden lures, silver spoons, bobbers, lead weights, and whetstone to keep his Case pocket knife super sharp. He also had a minnow bucket with live minnows and a box of worms he dug up from grandma's garden. Dad set up numerous rods and reels to fish from the lake's bank. He taught me how to bait a hook and fish from the bottom without a bobber. He also showed

My sister, Lanora Kelly and me, at five, in 1956, after catching a string of fish at Crystal Lake, Michigan.

me how to wait until the right moment after the bobber submerged to pull and reel in the line to properly hook the fish. Cleaning the caught fish was quite the chore. Holding the fish by its tail, we used a fish scaler to scrape downward towards the head, all the while attempting to avoid being finned. After scaling, we gutted the fish and cut off their heads. Then Dad dipped the fillets in egg wash and rolled them in cornmeal. Dad melted a stick of butter in a cast-iron pan to fry up bass, walleye, and perch.

I'll never forget the aroma and delicious taste—when we were able to eat them that is. Case in point, Dad caught a full stringer of large fish. Mostly sun-perch and large-mouth bass. Mom wanted him to place the fish in a bucket to keep the turtles away. But Dad wanted fresh fish to eat and thought they would die in the bucket before we could get home and clean them. So he tied the stringer of live fish to a stick on the bank and gently placed them back in the water, their tails and fins swishing around in the lake.

Thirty minutes later Dad pulled the stringer from the lake before heading back to Stanton. To his disappointment, all that was left were heads and bones. The turtles had eaten them all. Mom was right. The turtles were the only ones enjoying fresh fish that day.

As an excellent swimmer, Dad put me on his back as he swam in Crystal Lake. Using the "sink or swim" teaching technique, Dad tossed me off of his back, lifting me out before I took in any water. Being completely submerged was a new experience, but I learned to open

Front of a postcard, highlighting pictures of Crystal, Michigan, Grandma Williams sent to my Mom in 1938.

my eyes under water for the first time. When Lanora was four years old, she stood in the water holding on to the dock next to my mother, Vivian Williams Kelly. Mom told her not to let go or the waves would knock her down. Lanora released her hold and was washed under the dock. Mom's brother Lester answered her screams for help. Dressed in his Sunday best, including brand new shoes, he jumped into the lake and frantically searched for Lanora, using his hands since he was unable to see her in the dark murky water. Lester finally located her small body, dragged her from underneath the dock and performed CPR on my sister, saving her from drowning. Lanora remembers this near-death experience to this day.

Many lakeside amusement and entertainments were located at and near a giant pavilion on the Crystal Lake shore. The aroma of cotton candy, popcorn, hamburgers, and hot dogs permeated the summer air. We enjoyed homemade ice cream and ice cold soft drinks. Built in 1916 in North Tonawanda, New York, the Crystal Carousel was brought to Crystal, Michigan, by "Doc" Stuart in 1936. This merry-go-round with its elaborately painted carved wooden horses was a favorite activity for us kids. The calliope music could be heard clear across Crystal Lake. Bowling, roller-skating, dancing, eating establishments, fishing, swimming, and boat races were also popular at the Lake.

Throughout the years, entertainment also consisted of a ballroom for bands and dances. As a young woman, Mom went often to the palladium, dancing to either a local band or a more famous group passing through to their next show. Many small Michigan lakes had these pavilions. Clifford Lake pavilion was another place Mom liked to dance. Docks, diving platforms and parks were later added. Opening in the early 1900s, most closed during the '30s and '40s. I remember the pavilion at Crystal Lake when I was a kid in the 1950s and 1960s.

Mom packed picnic lunches for us to take to the lake. Peanut butter and jelly, bologna and potted meat sandwiches, Fritos or potato chips always tasted better if eaten outdoors. Sometimes we had cold chicken and potato salad. She also prepared a thermos of hot coffee. I remember drinking my first cup of coffee at three years of age. It was good with lots of sugar and cream added to it. My mother made excellent coffee.

We carried water in a large metal can. Dad chopped up large blocks of ice bought from the local ice house to keep the water cold. A stainless steel ladle with a wooden handle was used to dip water from the can. Many times we wrestled to see who drank first out of the silver dipper. None of us wanted to give up the dipper, because we wanted to drink out of it. The ice was slow to melt inside the water can, making it the best cold water I have ever tasted on a hot summer day. Fun times picnicking, swimming, and fishing at Crystal Lake.

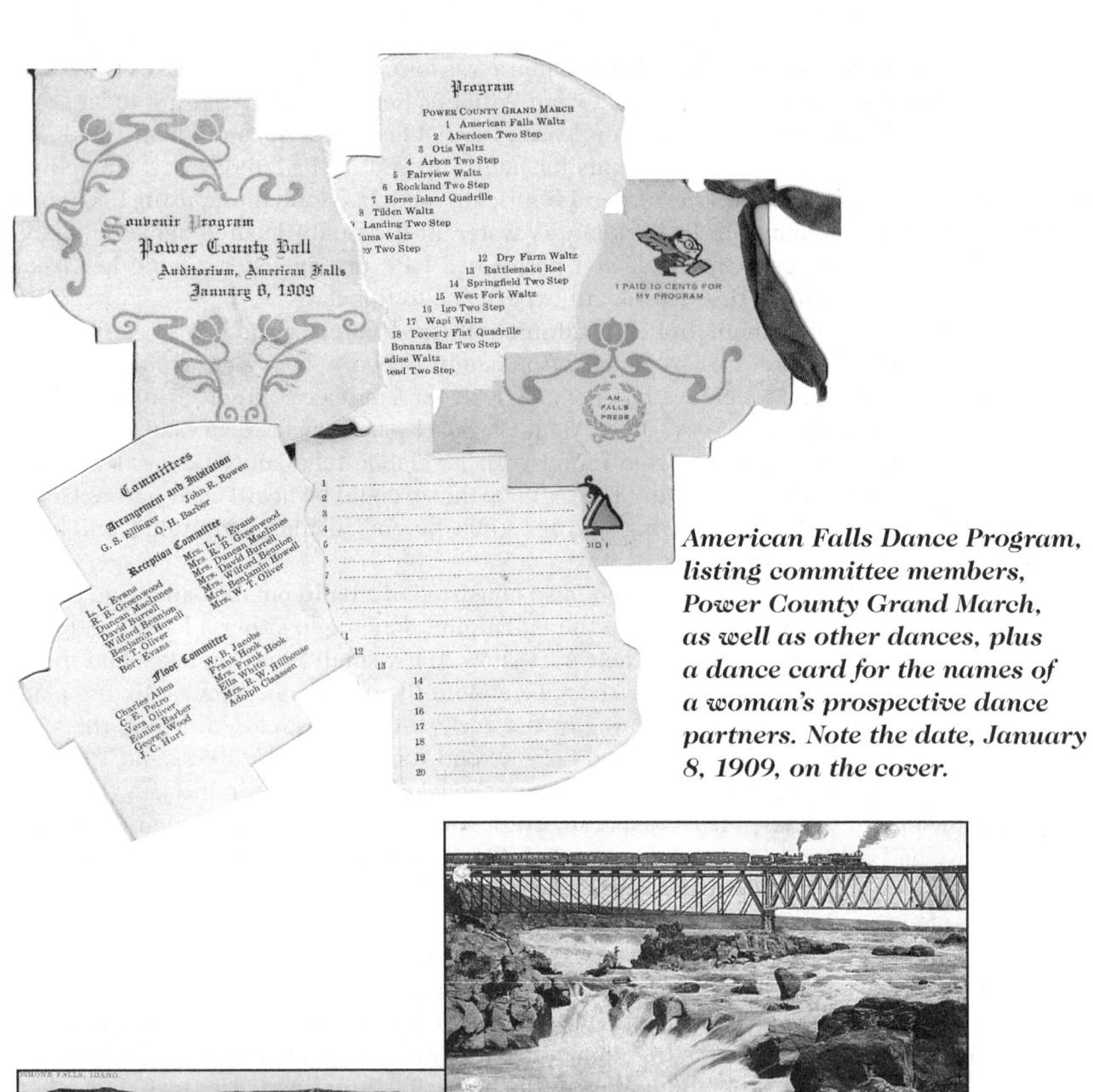

American Falls Dance Program, listing committee members, Power County Grand March, as well as other dances, plus a dance card for the names of a woman's prospective dance partners. Note the date, January 8, 1909, on the cover.

Vintage postcards of American Falls on the Snake River and Shoshone Falls, purchased by my grandmother when she lived in Idaho in the early 1900s. One of these cards was postmarked 1909 and was sent from Boise, Idaho, by Elnora Parrish Williams to her mother, Elizabeth Miller, in Stanton, Michigan.

Out West—1908

About 1908 my Delaware Moor grandma moved temporarily from Michigan to Boise, Idaho. Elnora Parrish Williams ran a restaurant near a hotel run by her sister, Carrie E. Parrish Bennett and husband Romaine M. Bennett. They lived close to American Falls, Idaho, for about two years, before moving back to Michigan in 1910. My grandmother gave my mother a souvenir dance program from the Power County Ball Auditorium, American Falls, Idaho, January 8, 1909. It had twenty-one different reels, waltzes, two steps, and quadrilles with lines for recording who you danced with (all blank). The program was small enough to fit in the palm of your hand and sold for ten cents. If this souvenir dance program from the past could speak, what fascinating stories it would tell of a moment in time from long ago.

My grandparents in their ranch house at the foothills of the Rocky Mountains near the Snake River, five miles outside of Boise, Idaho. Seated in the rocking chair is Lewis Milton Williams. To his immediate right is six-year-old Ruth Avalyn Williams. Seated in the chair is an unknown child. Seated at the piano is Elnora Parrish Williams.

Grandma Williams told a story when I was a little boy, about living on the edge of the Blackfoot Indian Reservation, near the Snake River, in the foothills of the Rocky Mountains, about five miles outside of Boise, Idaho. The Indians would sometimes get drunk and leave the reservation. These wild Indian warriors with war paint on their faces riding their barebacked, painted ponies, followed my grandmother as she drove a buckboard wagon down to collect drinking water at the river. As soon as she filled the water barrel, Grandma said the drunk Blackfoot Indians chased after the buckboard. She whipped the horses from the river to her ranch house, as arrows were wildly shot into the barrel, spilling water along the way.

She taught me a remedy learned from a Blackfoot Shaman. She made me lie back in a chair, inside a quiet dark room. I was instructed to close my eyes and visualize waterfalls, gentle rain, slow flowing rivers, lakes and pools within pools. Grandma had me gently rub my fingertips in a wavy motion over my forehead and shake them in a downward motion to remove the pain from my head. I repeated this over and over. In a short time, the pain disappeared. This ancient Indian remedy is now called a relaxation technique. To this day, I rarely get headaches. According to my mother, Vivian Madeline Williams Kelly Honea, Elnora Parrish Williams wrote a story for *True Story Magazine* in the 1940s about her adventures "Out West." The story reportedly received an honorable mention by this magazine.

Grandma's Letter—1964

Prior to and through most of the twentieth century, people wrote letters and postcards to communicate with their loved ones far away via the United States Postal Service. I consider letters to be windows into our past. Following is a letter written to me in 1964, when I was thirteen years old, from my wise Delaware Moor Grandma. In the letter she prophetically mentions: "I am looking forward to you being a great scholar and writing a book." Even in her eighties she was still articulate.

Stanton, Mich.

Dec. 11, '64

Dear Loren—

I received your letter and real happy to get it. I am so happy you are young as you are, as you can do so much for your parents, as you are the only one left at home. When they are feeling ill you sure can be a great first aide to them and so much as you are strong and so healthy and real wise for your young age. I am so glad for such a wonderful grandson. I depend on you and it relieves the burden I have on my mind, whenever I hear your parents are sick. I know Lanora does all she can, yet she is not always there.

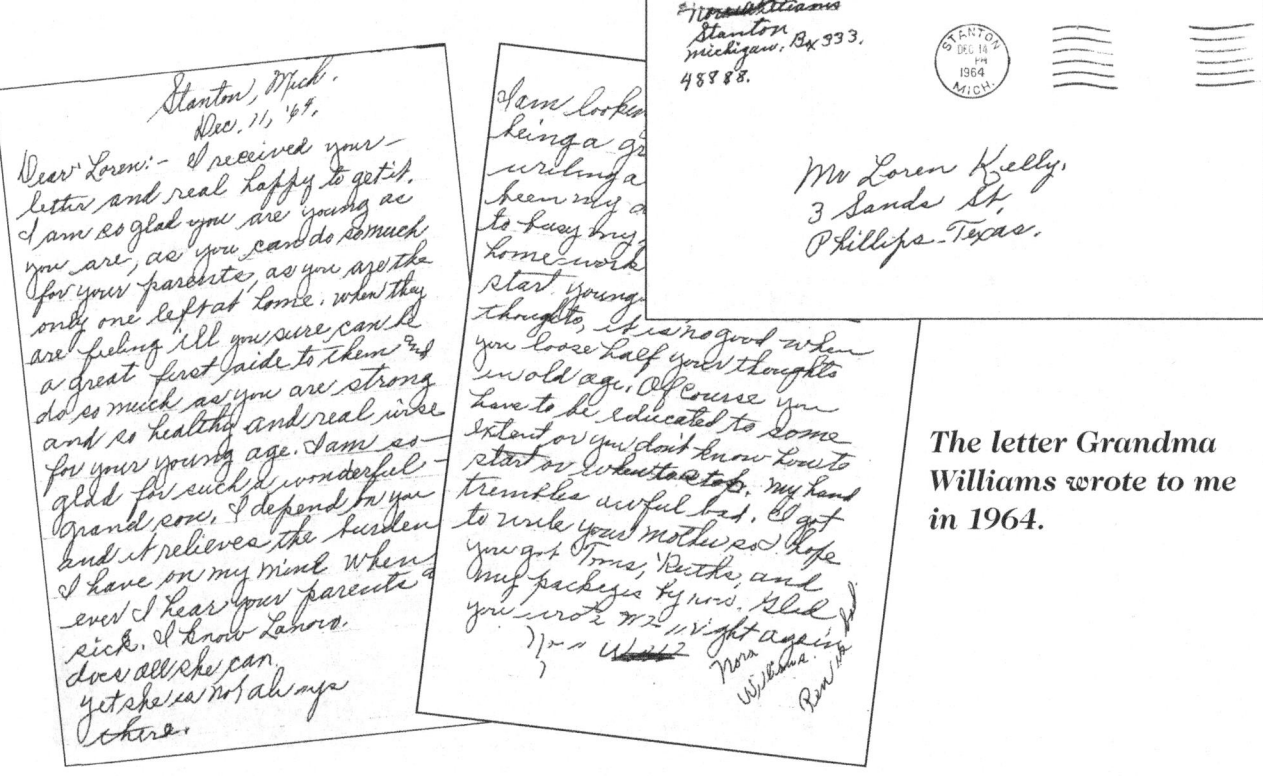

The letter Grandma Williams wrote to me in 1964.

This is Sunday evening and they have all gone to church. The ground was so slippery with snow. I felt more safe at Tom's house, so I did not attend. I suppose you attend every Sunday. First thing I know you'll be teaching a class. I hope you pass this year. I am sure you will. It's hard, but it's worth it in coming years. I was a good scholar and I had to quit school, as my father's health failed and I had to work and earn money to help my mother buy groceries—but what I learned I never forgot and it has been a great help to me ever since.

I am looking forward to you being a great scholar and writing a book. Writing a book has always been my desire, but I had to busy my hands in the home and work. And unless you start young in life on those thoughts, it is no good when you lose half your thoughts in old age. Of course you have to be educated to some extent or you don't know how to start or when to stop. My hand trembles awful bad. I got to write your mother. So I hope you got Tom's, Ruth's and my packages by now. Glad you wrote me. Write again.

Nora Williams (Pen is bad)

Grandma Williams, standing in front of her house in Stanton, Michigan, when she was in her eighties, about 1964

Long Lost Brother

After my mother's death on March 3, 1990, I discovered a letter, dated August 21, 1942, among her personal effects. The letter mentioned a divorce from a Ralph E. Williams and the legal adoption of John Thomas Williams, born December 21, 1934, in Plainfield Township, Kent County, Michigan. I also found a picture of Mom (Vivian Williams) sitting on a porch at her sister, Avalyn Ruth Williams Chorman's apartment at 2524 Plainfield Avenue in Grand Rapids, Michigan, taken about 1934. Written in pencil on the back was "126 pounds; worked at Millers." The penciled note on the back of the photo was evidence of pregnancy since my mother's normal weight at that age was 105 pounds. At that time, she lived with Avalyn and worked at Miller's Ice Cream Store. Mom was about sixteen years old. Shortly before she died, Mom had shown me the photo of a baby, which I later found among her things. Mom told me the picture was not of a real baby, but was a doll. I now believe the baby was my brother.

As a genealogist I wanted my brother to know he had other family members who loved him. For years, like a detective who never gave up on a cold case, I persistently searched for my long-lost brother. Further investigation uncovered the truth. On July 8, 1993, I spoke to my Uncle Clayton Williams, Mom's brother, on his seventy-third birthday. I asked Uncle Clayton if my mother had been married before and had a baby. Clayton gazed down at the floor with a sad look on his face and nodded yes. He explained he was young at the time, but was aware his sister had to go away in November of 1934 and suspected she was pregnant. He further advised her marriage was legitimate and she had gone to live with Avalyn in Grand Rapids. He also stated, "Avalyn was smart and fixed it!" In 1995 I discovered the strict adoption laws in Michigan had changed and I finally acquired the necessary adoption records from

(above) My mother, Vivian Williams, at about sixteen years old and pregnant with John, sitting on her sister's porch in Grand Rapids, Michigan (1934). (right) My brother John as a baby.

Kent County, Michigan. John Thomas Williams (Birth name) was adopted by Harold W. Morris (W.P.A. worker) and Lena M. Morris (nee Ketcham) of Grand Rapids, Michigan, on October 2, 1936. They gained custody on January 20, 1935, and legally adopted him on October 2, 1936. His adoptive parents changed my brother's name to John Warren Morris.

On February 15, 2009, I located what appeared to be prior addresses dating back to 1985. The last known address of my brother was in Sanford, Florida. After uncovering this information it did not take me long to discover what had happened. My long-lost brother was a Korean and Vietnam U.S. Army veteran. I searched for over twenty years and finally found him, but it was too late. John died one day after my birthday, less than one year before I finally located him. By the time I finally found my brother John, he was gone. It appeared he lived in Sanford, Florida, from August 2001 until his death on March 4, 2008. The unforgiving challenges of time delayed my search. Some things in life are never meant to be. I deeply regret I never had the opportunity to meet my brother.

My long-lost brother, John Warren Morris' (John Thomas Williams') gravemarker at Florida Veterans National Cemetery in Bushnell, Florida.

I discovered the telephone number for his ex-wife Peggy, who lived in, Palmyra, Tennessee. When I spoke to Peggy, she said he had joined the Army at eighteen and remained in the service for about 30 years. He entered the Army at Fort Campbell, Kentucky, and was a cook. His former wife further stated after the service he worked on oil rigs in Louisiana and Texas. Peggy said they had no children and were married about twenty years. He knew he was adopted and his real last name was Williams. She further advised that he was a loner and he always wanted to meet his biological mother. Peggy described John as a big guy at well over 200 pounds, and confirmed he died of a stroke in Sanford, Seminole County, Florida, on March 4, 2008. John is buried in the Veteran's National Cemetery in Bushnell, Florida. Peggy also stated John had always wondered if his mother ever loved him.

Learning that Mom's divorce decree alleged cruelty as the basis for her early divorce, that and being only sixteen, I instinctively knew Mom put John up for adoption out of love. If there had been any way for her to keep John, she would have done so. The situation must have been pretty awful for her to give up her first born child. I believe she didn't tell any of her other three children about our long-lost brother, because of the trauma and shame associated with putting a child up for adoption. I only uncovered this well-kept secret after her death. There is no doubt in my mind Mom loved John, because of how much she loved her other kids as well as the fact that she kept his picture and the letter about his adoption for forty-seven years.

I believe she wanted us to eventually know that we had an older brother somewhere out there, and subconsciously wanted us all to be reunited. It's regrettable that John never learned his birth mother certainly loved him, and that we never got to know our brother John.

Ma's Precious Secret

Just before my mother died on my birthday, March 3, 1990, I attempted to conduct genealogical research on her side of the family. She sternly stated; "Be careful. You just might find out something that you may not like." Even though I asked what she meant, she would not reveal what our family had held close to their hearts since the American Civil War. My mother's precious secret was she's of African and Native American heritage, Delaware Moor to be exact. Mother guarded her secret, cherished it, and knew like many precious things, it couldn't be freely shared. Some have suggested she may have felt some shame. True, she kept it silent, but this was something she loved and connected with people whom she loved. She was not ashamed.

Like family before her, Mother protected their secret from unkind and hateful eyes for more than four generations. The 1860 Delaware Federal Census, the last during the era of slavery listed her family as Mulatto. The Michigan Federal Census in 1870 and beyond listed her family's race as White. If this secret were exposed, her family would have come to great harm. I sensed it was fear and not shame that held her tongue when she alluded to the family secret before she passed. This was the only time she ever came close to revealing our secret. Although she knew she was so close to death, she still could not bring herself to tell me. She kept it from her children to protect her family from society's racial prejudice. There is no doubt in my mind she kept our precious family secret out of love for her children. It was the same with all of her family who knew the secret for over four generations. My mother and grandmother had a strong sense of family which was subsequently passed down to me.

Vivian Madeline Williams Kelly Honea at nineteen in 1936 in Oklahoma City, Oklahoma...

The Delaware Moors are a mixed-blood group of Native American, African American, and European American descent. Historian J. Thomas Scharf in his book, *A History of Delaware 1609-1888,* noted these so-called Moors recognized themselves and were recognized by their neighbors as a distinct ethnic group at least as early as the eighteenth century. Scharf described them as settling in Little Creek [now Kenton] Hundred

...and at sixty-eight in 1985 in Stanton, Michigan

Delaware about 1710. Scharf also mentioned an 1849 Delaware law which threatened to sell "idle and poor" free Blacks into servitude for a year if they remained unemployed. These laws resulted in a migration of Delaware Blacks northward during and after the 1850s, including my ancestors Enoch D. Miller and Phoebe Carney Miller (my maternal great-great-grandparents) and their daughter Elizabeth Miller Parrish.

Through genealogical research I uncovered the family's secret in 2004 while researching my mother's (Vivian Williams Kelly) maternal ancestral line. My maternal grandmother, Elnora Parrish Williams, was the daughter of Elizabeth Miller Parrish, born November 25, 1849, to Enoch D. Miller and Phoebe A. Carney Miller in Duck Creek Hundred, Kent County, Delaware. Phoebe A. Carney and Enoch D. Miller were descendants of the Delaware Moors, a Colonial Mixed-Race community. My family passed as White on every Census after the Civil War, giving them the legal right to vote, own a gun, not be sold into slavery and not be hung and left dangling from the end of a rope just because they were different. Mom and Dad kept this family secret so they would not be arrested and placed in jail for being involved in an inter-racial marriage, which was illegal in most states in America until 1968.

Michigan Twister

Tornadoes are an infrequent visitor to Michigan, compared to the twister-prone state of Texas. My parents and I lived in the Texas Panhandle, part of the infamous Tornado Alley frequented by numerous tornadoes on an annual basis. In the late '60s, when I was a teenager, we visited family in Stanton, Michigan. The Williams and Kelly families were gathered at Uncle Tom's preparing for a dinner of Aunt Winnie's famous goulash. A tasty dish I was looking forward to devouring. We were about to sit down at the kitchen table when we were startled by the booming voice of Stanton's local constable racing down the streets in his patrol vehicle. "Run. Take cover. Get into your basements. A twister is coming. Save yourselves," he repeatedly and frantically yelled through a bull horn he held out his car window. Michiganders are not known for understanding how to deal with tornado warnings and my relatives were no exception. Everyone began running amuck, yelling to themselves and at each other while trying to figure out what to do.

Dad and I remained seated at the kitchen table, amazed at the chaos. We calmly walked outside, looked up at the sky, and assessed the potential calamity. We didn't see any telltale signs of a twister. The air wasn't humid, the sky looked fairly clear with a slight breeze blowing. No rain, no hail, and no wall cloud in the sky. Nothing suggested a tornado was in the area. As we walked back into Tom's house, it was like an episode of the Keystone Cops. Uncle Lester, Uncle Clayton, and Uncle Tom were running into each other as they gathered and dropped flashlights, blankets, and pillows, folding chairs, a first aid kit, radio, and anything else they thought might get them through the foretold catastrophe. Uncle Tom yelled at the women and children to get down the basement steps, before they were whisked away by this supposed killer tornado. He frenziedly motioned to the basement stairs and kept saying, "Women and children first." It was almost like we were on the Titanic.

Uncle Tom Williams fiddling at his house in Stanton, Michigan, awaiting his wife's goulash.

While everyone else panicked and stumbled down the basement steps, Dad and I remained upstairs in the living room, occasionally looking outside for any signs of disaster. We both noticed, amidst the hysteria, Uncle Tom left eighty-plus-year-old Grandma Williams sitting on the living room couch. She was shaking and scared so Dad and I attempted to reassure her everything would be all right. After calming down Grandma, we heard Tom's bellowing voice from the basement. "Oh My God! We forgot Ma!" He and Uncle Lester ran up the stairs to help her into the basement. After a heated debate, both uncles decided to put Grandma in a chair they dragged from the kitchen. Picking her up like a sack of potatoes, they dropped her into the chair and piled blankets and pillows on her lap. You could barely see her head, but the look of fright on her face was unmistakable. Tom and Lester picked up the chair, with Grandma seated in it, and hurriedly carried her down the basement steps.

We could hear her crying out, "You're going to break my leg." Uncle Tom yelled back at her, "Better your leg getting hurt, than the tornado getting ya, Ma." After a few minutes Uncle Tom resurfaced from the basement on a valiant rescue mission to save the pot of goulash. Like a deer caught in a car's headlights, Uncle Tom begged us to hunker down in the basement with the rest of the family. Dad and I reassured him we would be all right and remained upstairs as diehard Texas scouts. At least the goulash was out of harm's way so we could have a last meal when the tornado hit. Dad and I couldn't stop laughing. Unlike in The Wizard of Oz, the monster tornado never materialized to pick up Uncle Tom's house and send it flying towards the Land of Oz.

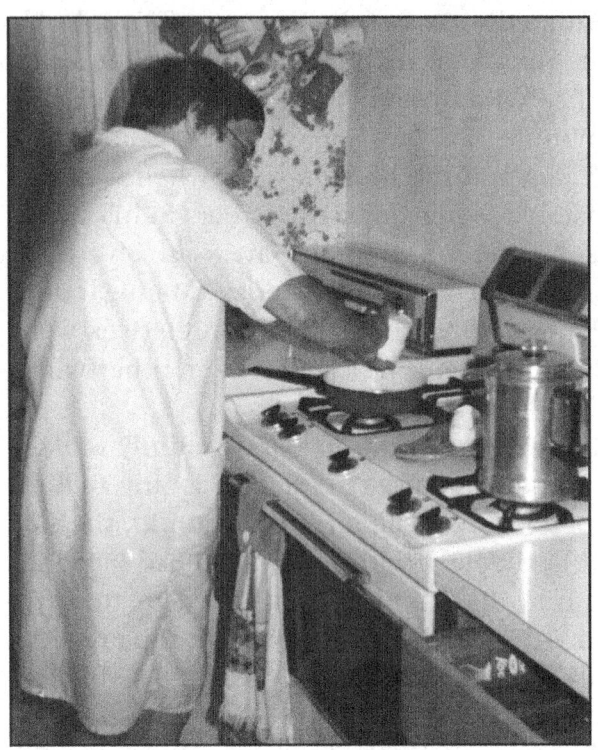

Aunt Winnie Williams at her house in Stanton, Michigan, prepping for her famous bowl of goulash.

Delaware Moor Warriors

Warrant Officer Private Thomas Milton Williams: D-Day and the Battle of the Bulge

I remember my Delaware Moor Grandmother Williams saying her two sons were saved by God from the mouth of the lion during World War II. They were not only Delaware Moor blood brothers, they were truly brothers in arms during World War II. Tom Williams served in the European Theatre during World War II. Enlisting in the Michigan National Guard, he was attached to and served in the 101st Airborne and flew into France in a glider during the Normandy D-Day invasion.

As troops were storming Utah and Omaha Beach, on June 6, 1944, Tom and a dozen other glider men infantry loaded into America's first military stealth aircraft, the Waco CG-4A combat glider, and silently soared into World War II history over seventy-six years ago. These gliders were nicknamed "silent wings" or "flying coffins," because they were powered only by the prevailing winds and the guts of the soldiers (with no parachutes) who flew in them. Just before dawn, under the veil of morning darkness on D-Day, engineless and unarmed, Tom's combat glider was towed by a C-47 tow plane. The fragile CG-4A fuselage was forty-eight-feet long and constructed of aluminum tubing and canvas skin. It had a thin honeycombed plywood floor. The Waco maxed out at 150 mph when connected to its tow plane. Once the three-hundrend-feet of one-inch nylon rope was cut, the gliding speed was reduced from 150 mph to a 72 mph average speed. Some of these glider pilots had washed out of conventional pilot training and were given a second chance to fly. Air pockets and 40 mph winds created violent turbulence.

These stealth gliders were totally silent and detection by the enemy was difficult, greatly increasing the element of surprise. Gliders were helpless against ground fire if they were detected before landing. Enemy fire on descent was constant, and many of the pilots were taken out before they could land. Landing a glider in com-

Pvt. Thomas Milton Williams, 101st Airborne

bat was a harrowing experience. Glider landings were quite often rough and brutal affairs, sometimes injuring or killing soldiers. Tom said his hard landing gave a man religion. About fifty percent of these tow targets crashed, or was shot down, but Tom's Waco was one of the lucky ones that managed to land. Over 3,900 glider-borne troop's mission were to disembark intact and combat ready in the designated landing zone (LZ) and fight behind enemy lines on D-Day. Tom overcame perilous odds to take a first crack at Hitler's Army. He jumped out of the glider armed with his M1A1 carbine to take out German defenses and transportation links.

Tom continued to fight the Germans for over 340 miles across Europe towards the Western front. About five months after leaving France he was fighting at the the Battle of the Bulge in the Ardennes Forest of Belgium. When I was a boy, I pestered Uncle Tom until he finally revealed one more story about his exploits, involving this battle at its worst moments. It was snowing hard as he drove a Willys jeep enroute to deliver dispatches to General Patton. Tom remembered shooting German soldiers crouched in the ditch on both sides of the slick ice-covered road with his 45-caliber sidearm as he drove like a bat out of hell to deliver those vital messages. Like most veterans of World War II, Uncle Tom did not normally talk about the war. As part of the Greatest Generation, he had completed his duty and returned home, without complaint, to work and raise a family.

Tom Williams' military hat, glider pin, and patches reflecting his service in the 101st Airborne.

Elnora Williams with her son Pvt. Tom Williams

Corporal Clayton Carlos Williams: World War II—Battle of Buna, New Guinea

Clayton Williams became a member of the armed forces on February 19, 1940. When war broke out on December 7, 1941, he was training with the Michigan National Guard as a private at Camp Livingston, Louisiana. He was a Squad Leader in the Battle of Buna, New Guinea, during World War II as part of the 32nd Red Arrow Division, 126th Infantry. He received the Asiatic-Pacific Campaign Ribbon with two Battle Stars and The Distinguished Unit Citation. Clayton served as a squad leader for a total of thirty-three months in the Southwest Pacific Theater of Operations and never liked talking about the war.

My Mother told me about one incident. At the Battle of Buna, New Guinea, the Japanese had been pushed into the sea. Both sides had run out of ammunition and food and were fighting and killing each other with rocks and sticks. The Japanese were cannibalizing the dead Australian soldiers. After crawling across the Owen Stanley Mountains—literally on his belly—he was lying wounded, lost in the Jungle, and was caked in mud and blood. His body was emaciated and his uniform was tattered and dirty.

An American Patrol found him, but he was so unrecognizable they thought he was a Japanese soldier and were about to shoot him before one of the patrol's soldiers stopped them. The soldier rubbed the mud and blood off of Clayton's tattered uniform and saw an American flag. The Stars and Stripes saved his life that day. He was hospitalized in Australia while recovering from wounds incurred in the Battle of Buna. Other than this one account he never talked about what happened to him in the Pacific. Like his brother, he was also a member of the Greatest Generation. He was a carpenter by profession, as was his father, and returned to that work, without complaint or bragging about how he fought for his country.

Pvt. Clayton Carlos Williams, Michigan National Guard at Camp Livingston, Louisiana.

Clayton Williams (second from left), recuperating after being wounded.

Private Otto Rollin Parrish: World War II—Battle of Hurtgen Forest

Grandma Williams' nephew Private Otto Rollin Parrish, son of her brother Arthur "Archie" Parrish, was in the United States Army, 110th Infantry Regiment, 28th Division, during World War II. He was not saved by God from the mouth of the lion and was declared "killed in action" in Oulder, Belgium, on Friday, October 5, 1945.

His burial is considered to be at Ardennes American Cemetery and Memorial at Neupre (Neuville-en-Condroz) Arrondissement de Liege, Liege, Belgium, and he is memorialized on the *Tablets of the Missing*. He was awarded the Bronze Star, a Purple Heart, and the European African Middle Eastern Campaign medal. Belgium also awarded him an Honor Pin.

In little more than a month after landing at the Normandy beachhead, as part of the Allied invasion, Otto and the 28th Division entered Paris and were given the honor of marching down the Champs-Elysées on August 29, 1944 in the Liberation of Paris. After enjoying a brief break from fighting, the division headed to the German defensive Westwall. The 28th Division struggled on the Siegfried Line at the Dragon's Teeth (fortification) infested Westwall. They crossed the Our River by bridge from Luxemburg into Sevenig (Our), Germany, making them the first of the Allied armies to reach German soil. The 28th suffered excessive casualties that autumn in the costly Battle of Hürtgen Forest. The fortifications there were massive and well-built. These structures, called "The Siegfried Line," were built originally in the 1930s and refortified in the '40s.

Tablets of the Missing (Liege, Belgium) showing Pvt. Otto R. Parrish, who was declared "Killed in Action" following the Battle of the Bulge in WWII.

Aimed at driving to the port of Antwerp through Luxembourg and Belgium, Hitler had launched his last military reserves in one last gamble, but the 110th Infantry, 28th Division, stood in his way. It was a forest battle with many soldiers maimed and killed by flying shards of wood as trees literally exploded from mortar fire during battle, giving rise to nicknames "the blood bucket" or "the meat grinder." The 28th Division dug into foxholes as they held a line through the Ardennes Forest against Hitler's army. Without the 28th Division's brave stand at the onset of the offensive, the 101st Airborne may not have reached Bastogne in time and the war would have been prolonged. The Battle of Hurtgen Forest was the longest battle on German ground during World War II and is the longest single battle in U.S. Army history. A book was written about their hardships called *The Lost Division*.

Otto died in the fall of 1944 during the battle of Hurtgen Forest, just before the Battle of the Bulge in which the 28th Division went in to relieve the 9th Division. Suffering so many casualties, they ceased to exist as a division with the highest casualty rate for one battle of the whole European conflict. He went missing in action at Oudler, Belgium, near the borders of Germany and Luxembourg in the fall of 1944, but was not declared dead until October 5, 1945. This is a customary military practice for soldiers missing in action or when their bodies could not be recovered, so their families could receive their VA benefits. Otto's unit was overrun in the Fall of 1944 and even the wounded were fighting. The Germans did not take prisoners before The Battle of The Bulge and killed everyone on sight, including Otto. I remember my mom, Vivian Williams Kelly, telling me her cousin Otto didn't come home from the war and the only thing Otto's family received were his charred dog tags.

Medals awarded to Pvt. Otto Rollin Parrish during WWII include the Purple Heart (far left) and Bronze Star (far right).

Private Dewitt Larue Parrish:
The American Civil War—Battle of Mobile, Alabama

Dewitt Parrish enlisted as a private into Company B of the Third Michigan Cavalry on February 23, 1864, at Canton, Wayne County, Michigan, for three years. He mustered into the service of the United States on February 24, 1864, at Detroit, Michigan. At the time of his enlistment he was twenty years old, 5'10" tall, with a light complexion, grey eyes, and brown hair. His occupation was listed as a farmer.

The Third Michigan Cavalry, Company B was closely identified with skirmishes and battles in the Southwest, including the Battle of Mobile, Alabama, and the surrender of the last troops under Confederate General Richard Taylor. During the surrender of the Confederate forces east of the Mississippi, Dewitt's regiment was selected as the escort to General Canby on the occasion of receiving the formal surrender of General Taylor's forces. Dewitt Parrish left Mobile on May 8, 1865, marching cross country reaching Baton Rouge, Louisiana, May 22, 1865. When General Sherman assumed command, the Third Michigan Regiment was selected to join an expedition to Texas.

My great-grandfather, Dewitt Larue Parrish (right). Both men are wearing "Slouch Hats," preferred by Union Civil War western armies. Dewitt Parrish is also wearing his Civil War cavalry blouse. It appears this particular photo, printed as a Post Card, was probably taken about 1866 in either San Antonio, Texas, or upon Dewitt's return to Michigan after mustering out at the end of the Civil War.

My great-grandpa, Dewitt Parrish, left Baton Rouge for Shreveport, Louisiana, on June 10, 1865, commencing the march into Texas and arriving at San Antonio on August 2, 1865. In September 1865 Dewitt Parrish was at the Quartermasters Department, but by November he was attached to General Stanley's headquarters in San Antonio. His duties included patrolling the general area, and guarding the Mexican border, where he performed garrison duty and was engaged in scouting until February 15, 1866.

Dewitt mustered out of the service on February 12, 1866, in San Antonio, Texas, with an hon-

Dewitt Larue Parrish as an older distinguished-looking gentleman. This Photograph was taken between 1905 and 1913, when he was in his sixties.

orable discharge after serving during the War of the Rebellion in the service of the United States. Muster out roll records indicated he was due the following: clothing account $49.54, arms and equipment $4.22, bounties of $180 and $120 Those same records indicated he was charged for one Carbine Screwdriver; one Thong and Wiper; one pair of lost Spurs and Straps; One Sabre and Accounts retained. According to records the Third Michigan served in ten states, occupying more territory and marching more miles than any regiment leaving the state of Michigan.

At forty-five years of age, Dewitt completed paperwork regarding a Declaration for an Invalid Pension on December 14, 1889. This pension application indicated he was partially disabled from obtaining his subsistence by manual labor for reason of deafness in both ears, caused by cannon fire during the fall of 1864 in the line of duty under the command of Captain F. C. Adamson at Brownsville Station, Arkansas.

After the Civil War, Dewitt and his brothers, William Roy Parrish and Charles Parrish were much in demand for local square dances. They played the fiddle, sang, and called the steps. Dewitt was born on February 7, 1844, in Canton, Wayne County, Michigan, and married Elizabeth Miller November 21, 1867, in Van Buren, Wayne County, Michigan. He was the son of Asa (b. February 20, 1815, in New York) and Mary Ann Coykendall Parrish. (b. February 20, 1821, in New York). They married April 21, 1839, in Canton, Wayne County, Michigan. Dewitt Parrish died at sixty-nine on November 9, 1913, in Stanton, Michigan, from a fall that injured his spine. His granddaughter, Vivian Madeline Williams Kelly Honea, told her children that Dewitt stubbed his toe and fell while walking in a potato patch.

Private Thomas Carney:
The American War of Independence—
Battle of Guilford Courthouse and Siege of Ninety-Six

One of my Carney ancestors, Thomas Carney was a corporal and free Black man in the American Revolutionary War. Thomas joined the Seventh Maryland at the start of the Revolution in May 1778. He served as a Continental Army private and corporal, fighting in some of the most iconic battles of the war—Brandywine, Germantown, Monmouth and Guilford Courthouse. Thomas not only fought at the Battle of Germantown, Pennsylvania, under General George Washington, but he also camped with Washington's forces during the frigid winter at Valley Forge.

Thomas did not lack for friends among both races. His obituary notice spoke of his friendliness and emphasized the cordial nature of his personality. He did not stand out in his company merely because of his friendliness or color, but from the fact that he was well over six-feet tall and noted for his great strength. Clearly in appearance and bearing he was quite different from the average soldier of the American Revolution.

Thomas Carney was still with the Marylanders in 1781 when his unit joined other American Continental units and the untrained ragtag North Carolina militia to confront the world's greatest army in the wilderness of central North Carolina. The battle site was in and around the little village of Guilford Courthouse. Patriot General Nathanael Greene posted the Maryland Brigade in a strong line between the North Carolina and Virginia militia. When the elite British Guards and the Marylanders collided, Carney valiantly cut down seven Redcoats in hand-to-hand bayonet fighting. The Second Maryland Brigade, commanded by Mordecai Gist and John Edgar Howard, boldly held its ground. They were sustained by their unshaken courage and three convincing bayonet charges. This brave and determined stand by the Marylanders in the face of the mighty British Army, allowed the rest of Greene's army to make an orderly withdrawal, saving it to fight again.

The American forces technically lost the battle waged which covered one thousand acres in what is now northwest Greensboro, North Carolina. But Greene's soldiers, including my ancestor Thomas Carney, killed and wounded so many of the enemy they effectively destroyed the British Redcoats as a fighting force. The English surrendered more than six months later at Yorktown, Virginia. It was indeed a victory in defeat. The Marylanders were some of the best of the American troops in the battle and were equal to or better than the British Army. With soldiers like Thomas Carney carrying the muskets this is no surprise.

Thomas Carney also fought at the Siege of Ninety-Six, from May 22 to June 18, 1781, when Continental Army Major General Nathaniel Greene led a thousand troops in a siege against 550 Loyalists in the fortified village of Ninety-Six, South Carolina. The twenty-eight-day siege centered on an earthen fortification known as Star Fort. Thomas was once again instrumental in the fighting, bayonetting more Red Coats. When company commander, Captain Perry Benson, was seriously wounded, Carney carried him a great distance to safety where surgeons attended him. Fainting from near exhaustion due to the intense heat and Benson's bulk, Carney put his own life at risk to save his commander. Captain Benson never forgot the act of heroism, and the two men later developed a lasting friendship. Whenever Benson, visited Denton, his first visit was to his brother-in-arms, Thomas Carney. Following the war, Benson served as commanding general of the Talbot and Caroline militia, and on muster days Carney was mounted at his side. In 1824 when French General Lafayette returned to America to meet one more time with those who had served with him fifty years before, Benson, with Carney again mounted and at his side, served as chairman.

After the war, Thomas Carney returned to farming in Maryland, He had fought for seven years in the Revolutionary War. The Denton Library shows that he received a postwar pension amounting to half his pay as an army private. Thomas received a cash bonus and one-hundred acres of bounty land for his service. This hero lived comfortably until advanced age made it difficult for him to earn a living. Help then came from the state legislature when General William Porter, delegate from Talbot County, introduced a bill to grant Carney a modest pension. Although the assembly was usually reluctant to act on such matters, the measure in 1813 passed by a unanimous vote. Several years later Carney's financial status improved when he received an additional pension from the federal government. This demonstrates that Thomas Carney was beloved as a war hero. His obituary tells of Carney's wartime gallantry.

Thomas Carney Revolutionary War Obituary

Thomas Carney, a colored man, aged 74, died near Denton, Md., 30 June. At the commencement of the Revolution, he enlisted as a soldier under Gen. Peter Adams, and soon afterwards was marched to the North, and was in the Battle of Germantown. In this action the Maryland Troops bore a conspicuous part, but the Americans were compelled to yield to a superior force. Soon after this, Washington retired to Valley Forge, and took up his winter quarters. When the Maryland and Delaware lines were ordered to the South, Thomas marched with his brave Regiment. At the battle of Guilford Court House he bore a conspicuous part, and bayoneted seven of the enemy when the Maryland Troops came to the charge. At Camden, Hobkick's hill, and Ninety-Six, he bore his part. At Ninety-Six, his captain (the late Major General Benson) received a dangerous wound. Thomas took him on his shoulders to the surgeon, and after laying him at the surgeon's feet, fainted from fatigue and heat.

—National Intelligencer Vital Statistics, 22 July 1828.

Memorial to the Maryland soldiers who fought at the Battle of Guilford Courthouse, Greensboro, North Carolina. The Maryland granite bears the inscription:

"Maryland's tribute to her heroic dead. Erected by members of the Maryland Historical Society in memory of the soldiers of the Maryland Line. 1781-1892. Non Omnis Moriar (I shall not wholly die.)
—Horace, a Roman lyric poet"

The historical monument stands in the Guilford Courthouse National Military Park.

My grandpa, Lewis Williams, sitting beside his house, smoking a cigar in Stanton, Michigan, 1960.

CHAPTER IV

Delaware Moor Family Poems

Phoebe Carney (Libby) Miller and Enoch D. Miller, my maternal Delaware Moor great-great-grandparents.

Delaware Moors

My people are forgotten folk
Known as the yellow men
Socially isolated Delaware farmers
Moorish descendants of mixed-heritage

Law-abiding tri-racial ancestors;
Black, Native American, White
Linked by kinship and marriage
To their mixed-blood community

Struggling as different races, but remaining free men
Indian River Indians of the Delmarva became invisible
By intermarrying with Black and White colonials
Avoiding forced assimilation

Racial islands unto themselves, refusing to pass for White
Almost White, but not, claiming to be totally Black
Blended remnants of Native American blood
Social outcasts sharing a common bond

A pre-colonial group of families
Labeled mulattos and free persons of color
They have survived for centuries
Keeping their culture and history alive

This is my family, a mixed-race fellowship
Proud and noble freedmen and women
United by love and history
Such are the Delaware Moors

February 23, 2019

The Parrish sisters: (bottom upward) Maude Ella Parrish Kunz, Lettie Dell Parrish Scoby, Elnora Parrish Williams (My Grandma), Emma Parrish Miller and Carrie (Cad) Parrish Bennett

Racial Epitaphs

Here lies my hidden family figures
These are my people
Living in chosen exile
Passing to keep their secret

They wanted to sail into freedom
Rather than buried in darkness
To survive in unlimited opportunity
Instead of dying in oppressive tragedy

I am the elegy of what has gone before
Which pays tribute to my cultural identity
Soulful Black blood, the intrinsic worth of self
Perfect whiteness is not who I am

When high-class means looking away
You destroy your low-class familiar
Creating the loss of ancestral past
And the invention of false present

Casting a cold eye on invisible genes
Even amidst flames of history
Passes racial essence by
And dishonors those left behind

Blessed be the man who recognizes who he is
Cursed be he who buries himself in the dust bin of time
A man's life struggle goes beyond the shackles of blood
And when he lies about who he is, becomes but a faded memory

February 17, 2019

Vivian Madeline Williams Kelly Honea (right), my Delaware Moor Mother, standing next to her best friend, Margaret Hanson, in 1940s Stanton, Michigan.

A Mother's Secret

My mother, living with fear, not shame
Family mystery not to be shared freely
Protecting little ones from unkind and hateful eyes
Never to reveal her blood secret

Southern Black codes of hate
Forced my people to flee
Hiding in the North Country
Invisible to persecution

Passing on the Census of time
A masquerade, undiscovered
Never vanquished at the end of the rope
To prevail and survive the struggle

Emerging from Jim Crow darkness
Tolerance forthcoming to ethnic difference
My family has finally overcome
A testament to mother's secret

Mother, a heroine to me
Not revealing her secret
Saving my soul from venom of contempt
Never to confess, she took it to the grave

Me, the youngest, uncovering the family secret
At the right time, before it is too late
To share with my children's children
So proudly, the truth of who we are

February 28, 2019

My daughter, Rachel Anne Kelly, as a little Girl, rocking in the family rocking chair as Grandma Vivian Williams Kelly Honea looks on at her House in Fritch, Texas, in 1988.

Rocking Chair

Rock me Mama in your old time rocking chair
Sleepy moments rocking backwards and forwards
As you held me so gently in your loving arms
Until my feet dragged on that hardwood bedroom floor

A mother's light shone on every baby rocked in this small rocking chair
A glow bright enough to light many an infant and toddler
Baby smiles and laughter caused by a mother's cuddling and tickling
From sons, daughters, and grandchildren rocked in that ole' rocking chair

Mother singing softly to the tune of "Stardust Melody" on her music box
Me, swaddled in a baby blanket, while nestled on Mama's lap
My baby eyes fluttering and finally closing in that old rocking chair
Ma kissing my brow and sweeping the baby curls from my warm forehead

Dear Mom of mine, I so wish you could still rock me in that rocking chair
As I watch my granddaughter smiling and swaying in our rocking chair
Realizing this timeless rocking chair represents years of many a mother's love
Reflecting affectionate mother and grandmother memories that will never die

Rocking our babies from antebellum Delaware to present-day Texas
This little Pennsylvania-made rocking chair passed through six generations
From a nineteenth century Delaware shack to a twenty-first century rural Texas home
Swaying many a tiny babe to sleep from the Civil War through the Afghanistan War

In my old age, as I look at that empty rocking chair
Yearning for and wondering why my mother's love had to leave me
Coming to an understanding that her loving arms are not gone
But are waiting still in heaven's golden rocking chair

October 23, 2019

Lewis Milton Williams (my maternal grandfather), Elnora Parrish Williams (my maternal Delaware Moor grandmother), Ruth Avalyn Williams (my maternal aunt) out west on horseback in front of a livery stable in Boise, Idaho, about 1908.

Roots

Ethnic heritage hides in underground places
Their origins removed to remote areas
Seeking transformation and social apartheid of the soul
Forced to exist in history, separated one from the other

Cultures, traditions, and customs disappear
When Black and Red Blood is excluded
White only, begets ghettoization
And erases the identity of difference

No diversity of people in their time
Is a catalyst for dead metaphors
Being absent of heart is a utopian myth
Meaning only the victors of life survive

Growing the branches of your community tree
Causes the fruit of your loved ones to blossom
Knowing where their root source is located
Defines their inherited traits and life stories

I am more than I thought I was
And knowing where I come from
Reveals my ancestors want to be found
Yielding a connection between generations

Passing down tribal adventures, a sense of kinship
My clan's exploits constitute a strength of purpose
Roots of my loved ones are a legacy
To be watered and nurtured in my Family Tree

February 21, 2019

The Parrish girls, my maternal Delaware Moor great-aunts, enjoying ice cream on a Sunday afternoon.

Not Forgotten

Beneath the surface of my ancestors
Lurks the shadows of Delaware Moors
Traits and customs surviving colonial times
My African and Indian lives of the past

Indian knowledge of not disturbing the buzzard's nest
Awareness of how to avoid great misfortune
Peculiar legends within superstitions
A pictorial saga of family heritage

Weather folklore of Indian River nature
Sassafras tea and herbal cures of Indian descent
Log and tree limb animal traps handmade with wooden tools
Passing beliefs of times gone by

Big Thursdays, an annual family affair
Our tribe coming together in all-day big crowds
Picnicking, horseshoe pitching, dancing, wrestling, boxing, and foot races
Traditions long lost to family feuds

Church gatherings, birthday celebrations, bingo games, and box socials
Social groups at talent nights of spiritual songs, and makeshift bands
Faithful homecoming day suppers honoring Moor families at Sunday services
Such were our get-togethers of winter Sunday dinners and summer Sunday picnics

Precious family secrets held in reverent memory
A dynasty bound by strong and noble unending ties
A lost parallel isolated world, because of racial intolerance
Origins, long ago and far away, but not forgotten

February 27, 2019

Myrtle (Myrtie) Parrish and her husband, Seymour Parrish, my great-aunt and great-uncle

CHAPTER V

American Revolution and Civil War Delaware Moor Poems

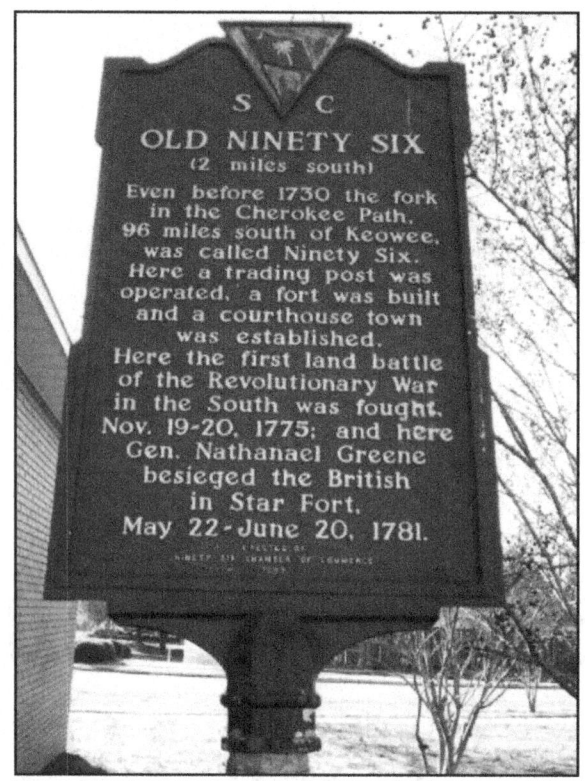

South Carolina Memorial for Old Ninety Six. Here, during the Revolutionary War, Thomas Carney, a free Black man, and his Second Maryland Regiment, besieged the British and loyalists at Star Fort. It was at this battle that he saved his seriously wounded White Captain, Perry Benson's life by carrying him off the battlefield. They became lifelong friends

Freejack Patriot

A Revolutionary War hero of the Battle of Guilford Courthouse, North Carolina, 1781
The first to charge, valiantly cutting down seven British Redcoats in bayonet fighting
Over six-feet tall and of great strength, a free Black man, admired by his comrades in arms
Such was the bravery of warrior Thomas Carney, enabling his compatriots to fight another day.

When the Second Maryland regiment, fiercest in the American Army, came to the charge
Soldier Thomas Carney did his duty for freedom, despite being denied future citizenship status
His bravery bore a conspicuous part of the Patriot army rallying troops for the ultimate win
British General Cornwallis never again to challenge Patriot General Greene in the Carolinas

Amidst the Revolutionary war "Siege of Ninety Six," South Carolina
Once again, the fate of our nation hanging in precarious balance
Maryland freedman, Thomas Carney, fighting in fierce hand-to-hand combat
Lunging at attacking Redcoats with bayonet and clubbing them with his musket

General Greene's sharpshooters firing into Star Fort at the British and Loyalists
Flaming arrows hurtling through a war torn sky into the enemies fortified position
Marylander, Thomas Carney, a Delaware Moor freejack, lunges over the redoubt
To recover the seriously wounded White Captain Perry Benson

Private Carney lifting his captain onto his shoulders and staggering to safety
Scaling stockade walls as musket balls and cannon shot whizz around him
Carrying his bulky burden through southern heat into the surgeon's tent
Laying Captain Benson's body at the surgeon's feet and collapsing from exhaustion.

White officer and Black soldier developed a lasting friendship, brothers in arms
Thomas Carney, my Delaware Moor ancestor, a freejack skirmishing combatant
Serving with George Washington at the Battle of Germantown, Pennsylvania, and Valley Forge
Snatching victory from defeat, a courageous fighting force to be reckoned with

March 3, 2019

Dewitt Larue Parrish (my maternal great-grandfather) At twenty years of age in his Union Blue Third Michigan Cavalry Uniform, he mustered into service at Detroit, Michigan, on February 24, 1864.

Dewitt Parrish's tombstone at Forest Hill Cemetery in Stanton, Michigan. As a young boy, I remember marching down main street in Stanton and up the hill to the cemetery on Memorial Day. I would sit on the cannon balls, stacked near my great-grandpa's grave as veterans fired a twenty-one gun salute.

Freedom

Progenitor's red blood stirred with Union blue and Confederate grey
Winds of Civil War unfurl enemy flags amidst cannon fire and soldier corpses
Resounding noises of rival armies fighting until their deaths win the day
Such are the rivalries that make freedom ring

The essence of any man is the power of independence
Equality is a heavy burden, borne by us all
Responsibility of duty to self-worth for the ultimate good
A universal quality of human freedom, realized

Sovereignty is what my forefathers fought for
Refusing to surrender in the dawn of their lives
Finding autonomy and self-determination
Discovering nothing hinders their yearning to be free

Godspeed to me and mine
My forebearers to be freed
My descendants to remain free
And the understanding that there is no other way

Mixed-bloods no longer enslaved by cruel masters
Mixed-heritage no longer restrained by overseers of hate
Mixed-race no longer exploited because of one drop of Black blood
I am free…unchained and released

Free from injustice and oppression
Free from penalties and pain
Free from confinement and suffering
Released from the shackles of slavery…I am Free.

February 25, 2019

A hero's grave. Debricks Miller, 34th New Jersey Union Infantry, Company D, (my Delaware Moor great-great-great-uncle), son of Phoebe (Libby) Carney Miller and Enoch D. Miller.

Glory

Glory to mixed relatives, known and unknown.
I pay homage to those who struggled on my behalf
Connected by circumstances of birth and life events.
Praising them for hanging the moon and stars of my beginnings

Lost worlds of ancestral epic adventures
Have painted the canvas of my very spirit
Overtures to family orchestral compositions of saints and sinners
A prelude to war and peace on the face of reality

My kindred offspring, forever on the run from timeless yesterdays
Engulfed by emotional storms faded into the eternal void of mystery
Lost, trying to find my way through the blood of my tribe
Surrounded by sense of self and deserted promises of unknown places

Folk flourishing in spaces called their own; a place called home
Wanting to escape themselves so their roll call can become complete
They think they all know, but know nothing they do
And only one is worthy to stand to honor his kind

Absolute rulers find it good to be King
Royal blooded sons dispute a rightful King
Sanctified heirs of the Kingdom sacrificial pawns falling on swords
Progeny down on bended knee, such a reverent sight to see

The pain of mulatto kin's deeds will become my past
There will be rejoicing in family revelations of who we are
But first I have to drink from the well of elusive tomorrows
My eyes wide open to see; I say glory be to me

February 21, 2019

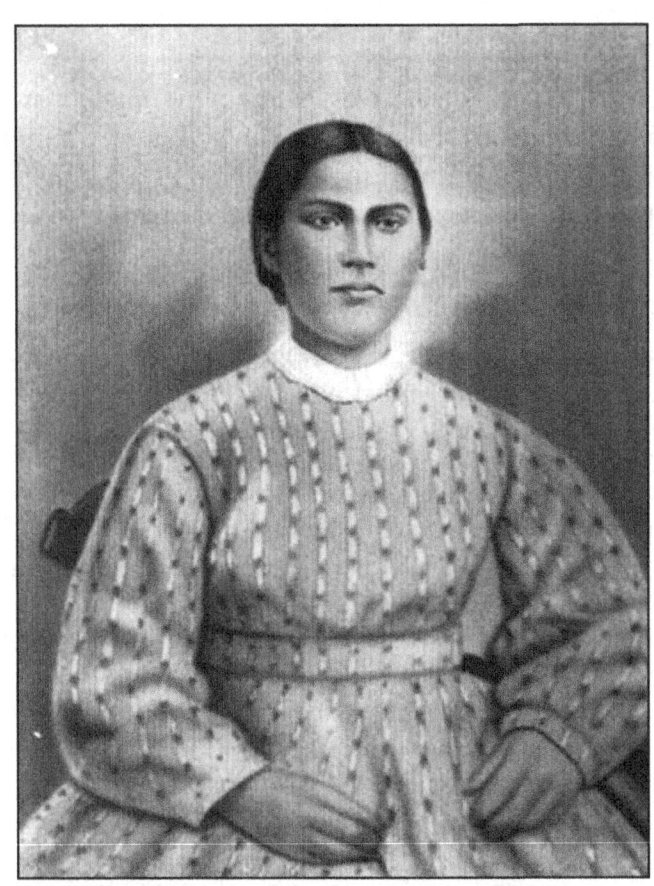

Prudence Sammons Concealor. A drawn portrait of her, dating back to the eighteenth or nineteenth century. She is one of my Delaware Moor ancestors, married to Edward Concealor and was the daughter of Benjamin Sammons and Sarah Miller. She appears to be wearing a cotton slave dress and could have been a slave at one time.

Slave

Treated as a wild animal
Sold as mere owned property
Subservient to the plantation master
Struggling in sweat and toil

Slave owners of historic oppression
Misbegotten illegitimacy of another time
Unrepentant devils of unbridled hate
Decaying in a cesspool of Civil War antiquity

Once enslaved in Darkness
Fleeing toward the Light
Absconding drudgery in servitude
Praying for freedom by slipping away

Standing by the river's edge
Crossing to a shameless safe-house
Steering clear of the fugitive's noose
Searching to be free from the rope's end

An agent conductor abolitionist escape route
A shepherd guide supplying tickets to passengers
Passing way stations as cargo through stationmasters
For a runaway slave's ride on The Underground Railroad

A realization of a long awaited dream
Liberty and self-determination
Never to be exploited as chattel, ever again
The gateway to that of freedmen

February 23, 2019

David West and my cousin David Chestnut, standing in the entryway to a plantation home as Civil War re-enactors of a Confederate soldier and a southern gentleman.

Plantation

Slave trade ships deliver chained African human cargo to a different shore
Masses of dark captives victimized for centuries in an oppressive land
Former proud princes of Africa become mere enforced labor
Relegated to sweat and toil of dirty tobacco fields, harvesting an evil crop

Forcibly dragged from homelands trapped in a slave pen on a dock
A once free people branded with hot irons, identifying wretched souls
Bodies washed and covered in grease and tar, creating a healthy image
Fetching as much money as possible and sold to the highest bidder

Auctioneers walk the enslaved up and down, like dogs, on the auction block
Human merchandise poked, prodded, opening mouths, like horses for sale
At the racecourse only the strongest and healthiest sold, split apart from children
Inspected like livestock as cheap labor, used and abused, sold into unending slavery

Ensnared family folk, separated and continually sold as slave owners valued property
Wallowing in the dirt of one room slave quarters on aristocratic fertile land
Crude hot boxes of the less respected, shadows of the master's plantation house
Ruled by the lash in villainy, dominated by immorality, until their lives end

Wicked monarchs of colonialism pose as southern landed gentry
As stolen King Cotton flows throughout their hate-filled landscape
Evil overseers fearfully whip dark seas of enslaved humanity
While refined plantation owners reap their repulsive rewards

White men owning Black men
Assaulting their lovely women indiscriminately
Using the whip to punish the undeserved
Such are the unpardonable sins of a suffering Southland

February 23, 2019

A restoration of the Dutch Slave Ship Leusden. *One of the last slave ships of the West-Indian Company (WIC). From her maiden voyage in 1719 until she floundered in 1738, amounting to ten crossings in total. During those ten voyages, 6,564 captives were embarked; 1,639 of whom did not survive the crossing. An additional 102 captives perished in the slave stores prior to being sold, resulting in an overall death count of 1,741. This proportion constituted more than a quarter of the number of captives embarked in Africa; an incredible waste of human lives. Its final voyage ended in the single largest human tragedy in Dutch maritime history. The ship wrecked at the mouth of the Maroni River at Suriname in 1738. At the time of the disaster there were still 680 captives on board. A mere 16 of them survived. The way in which the crew sent the remaining 664 African captives to their deaths is unimaginable, even considering the inherent cruelty of the slave trade.*

Slave Ship

A slaver packed full of six-hundred Africans underway thirty days off the coast of Africa
Slaves stowed so close together, wedged between each other's legs
Unable to lay down, impossible to sleep, struggling to extricate themselves
The first mate tossing the sick and feeble overboard

A ferocious slave driver threatening in the hatchway
Branding Black souls like sheep with owner marks, using a red-hot iron
Brutally burning dark flesh under female breasts and atop male arms.
Beating protesters with the flesh-ripping cat o' nine tails

Unwilling passengers, emaciated creatures, including children, near death
Crammed into small spaces merely three-feet high, shut out from light or air
Chained to the decks by the neck and legs, manacled in twos or threes, absolute captivity
Burning up in stifling heat; suffering in filth and misery, invisible souls

When carried onto the deck, many cannot stand
Shrieking, struggling, fighting for a single drop of water
Foaming at the mouth in their last agonies
Growing rabid at the sight of precious liquid

Suffocating nude wretches in desperation's final stages
Men strangling each other; women driving nails into each other's brains
Unfortunate creatures taking the first opportunity to leap overboard
Ridding themselves of intolerable lives

Dying men and women, companions of the dead
The living dead, crying out for their devil's nightmare to end
This evil commerce of humanity transforming into inhumanity
A deathly slave ship that will only heave to, at the fringes of Hell

February 26, 2019

Araminta "Harriet" Ross Tubman, my eighth cousin twice removed, conductor on the Underground Railroad, Union spy, army scout, nurse, suffragist, and military leader. Her friend, White abolitionist John Brown called her "The General." Assisted by Quakers, Harriet Tubman led more than three thousand slaves through Delaware to freedom. She was born into slavery in early 1822 in Dorchester County, Maryland, and died at 91 in 1913 in Auburn, New York. She was buried with military honors.

I had reasoned this out in my mind, there was one of two things I had a right to, liberty or death; if I could not have one, I would have the other.

—Harriet Tubman

Black Moses

Dedicated to Harriet Tubman my eighth cousin twice removed.

Dropping to her knees in a southern swamp
Her seizures, visions guided by God
Following the North Star to freedom
A Black Moses freeing her people

Her story lives within my DNA
A Civil War heroine accomplishing the unbelievable
A most extraordinary woman of color
An inspiration to never let anyone tell you what you can't do

A fearless abolitionist standing up for those who could not stand
Taking her people with her to freedom land
A guerilla fighter who fought for Liberty or death
Realizing if she couldn't have one, she would have the other

A conductor on the Underground Railroad
Evil slavers chasing her freed slaves
Their barking dogs tracking runaways
Fleeing bondage, as they wade in a river to live free or die

First woman in American history to lead U.S. troops in an armed assault
Commanding one hundred and fifty Black Union scouts in the Combahee River Raid
Torching plantations and liberating over seven hundred and fifty slaves
Vanquishing southern South Carolina slave owners

Harriet Tubman, fugitive slave, nurse, Union spy and army scout
Dedicating her life to helping freed slaves and women's suffrage
Deliverance was leading the way for her people to be free
Harriet's last words: "I go to prepare a place for you"

April 25, 2020

Vivian Williams Kelly, my mother, standing beneath the green apple tree at the side of her parents' house in Stanton, Michigan, 1952.

CHAPTER VI

Mixed-Blood Poems

My Delaware Moor great-aunt, Maude Ella Parrish Kunz. She was the most beautiful and the youngest of the Parrish Girls.

Mixed Messages

People glance in confused blindness
What secret face do they wish to see?
To what narrative do they think I belong?
My skin does not match who I know I am

DNA won't let me forget
Oceans of color crossed within me
A conspicuous outside does not belie the unseen
A claim to all my admixtures

The intertwining of disparate cultures
Identity is not a mere curiosity
I don't owe anyone a final answer
My ethnicities are entirely mine

Not a genetic puzzle of distinct chaos
No one breaks me down, to validate me
Overlap betwixt and between, layered and complex
Living body and soul, embracing all my parts

The landscape of selfless physicality
The mixed-blood forebearers you do not see
Accesses multiple racial epitaphs and past history
Belonging to myself and family, but to no other

Seeking to erase the persistence of my human uniqueness
Because I don't conform to what they expect
No assimilation; dilution threats resisted
Entirely something else, I am ancestral multitudes

February 17, 2019

My Delaware Moor mother, Vivian Madeline Williams Kelly, nineteen years of age, at her apartment on Classen Boulevard in Oklahoma City.

Labels

Labels put people back into chains
The dog leash of humanity
A pitfall for the good protagonist to avoid
A formidable foe for the victimized uninitiated

Mixed-race faces are merely observed traits
Inconsistent with what lies underneath
Believing is perceiving, but not seeing
We are all human, not to be defined by race

Race haters promote ghettoized destruction and offense
Race baiters genuflect to stereotypes, mislabeling those who aren't racist
Shame on social actors who seek to divide us
Bowing down to the unjust in a divinity of deceptive inequity

Labels shape false perceptions of human kind
Their hurtful nature causing great misunderstanding
Rejecting them is necessary, because not everyone fits
Not everyone is part of a common world view

Creating nonpartisan views in the eyes of the beholder
Behold, not one should see skin color when speaking of race
Shared experiences will educate the most uninformed
Love will see us through, God will make us more whole

Categorizations are not merely marionettes controlled by others
Action figures display the reflections of disparate cultures
Fighting the harmful effects of a social construct, know that race IS
My ethnicity is unidentifiable, yet exists, not to be labeled, but to be honored

February 23, 2019

My maternal Delaware Moor Grandmother, Elnora Parrish Williams, in her sixties, wading in Holland Lake, Michigan.

Exclusion

Being excommunicated from social norms
And relegated to the fringes of society
Establishes a mixed-race man irrelevant
As he becomes a ministry of intercultural conflict

Removal from the land of human dignity
Causes ostracism through social rejection
Promoting social control and invisibility
Of second-class citizens drowning in alienation

Hate speech for the sole purpose of labeling hate
Creates a caste culture of oppression
By blacklisting isolated individualism
Facilitating false impressions of social stigmas

So who are these excluded ones?
Are they embryo hybrids of mixed-blood?
Are they singled out, due to natural selection by phenotype?
Or do Black, White and Other selfish genes make them untouchable?

Human kind is more complex than you think
Denial and exclusion when humans conform and act the same
Acceptance and inclusion when humans do not conform and act differently
Inclusion and exclusion can be mutually one and the same.

Mixed-blood creates a genetic hero of human descent
Who survives or fails in DNA's primordial soup
An embargo against bias, resulting in removal of injustices
Injustices are not mere villains, but are mutated exclusions

February 25, 2019

Carrie "Cad" Parrish Bennett and Maude Ella Parrish Kunz (my maternal Delaware Moor great-aunts).

Folk

Old folk Delaware Moors; keepers of mixed-race traditions
Sources of White darkness and Black light
Both dwell within as a forever reminder
Chronicling the customs of ancestral people

Folk-tellers narrate the archives of racial inequities
These teller of tales are inhabitants of my genes
Family predecessors are bards of what has gone before
Stirring rousing memories of what is inherited

Alienated lineal fringes of relations are handed down
What runs in my family is undeniable historical ambiguity
The poorest of the poor versus the wealth of the evil elite
Is the disparity between my Black and White

Racial angst the real fear factor
Show me, don't tell me, a righteous mantra
Against hostile judgements and mindless biases
Becomes the marker of one's belief

The likeness of who I am is an outline in ebony and ivory; a testament to my paradox
A portrait of many faces, cut from the same fabric and interwoven in time
Innermost contours are blacked out in magnificent shadow against a lighter background
I am but a jagged silhouette appearing and disappearing in a lifetime

Deep-rooted in what is inborn, I become the storyteller
Bequeathed with what diversity really means
Inbred to be unorthodox with the passion of a reciter of tales
I am folk, delineating those shadows between antecedent love and hate

February 22, 2019

My maternal Delaware Moor great-aunt Maude Ella Parrish Kunz, wearing a swimsuit and combing her long beautiful hair.

Multi-Racial

Both Black and White…
Both Native American and White
No need to choose which one to be…
Nothing more, nothing less

Perception is not everything
What people perceive is not always the truth
And what people perceive is not always right
The truth and what is right lies in who we are within

There is much more than what you see on the outside
What you see on the inside truly defines who we are
My outside appearance is that of a white person; but I am much more
I celebrate what I am inside; Black and Native American

Interracial people are not one or the other;
But of all races/cultures/heritages
Acceptance of who we really are is the key…
Not how others want to describe us

I refuse to be identified by anyone's standards
I am other and I am all of the above!
I live individually or as the sum of all my parts
I am Multiracial!

May 16, 2010

Lanora Kelly, Lewis Williams, Suzanne Williams, Vivian Kelly holding Loren Kelly, Elnora Williams, and Richard Kelly outside Grandma Williams' house in Stanton, Michigan

CHAPTER VII

'Passing' Poems

Elizabeth Miller Parrish
(My maternal Delaware Moor great-grandmother)
as a younger woman.

One Drop

I have lived a secret life of passing;
the blood of descendants unknown.
Am I a stain on humanities soul,
because of the hidden blackness?

Serving an indeterminate sentence
not knowing my Black side.
Why do I have invisible genes,
maternal mulatto mixed with paternal White?

One drop is all that it takes
to be different from the rest.
Am I very White
or a little Black?

Doubters shout, you are not who you are,
because your one drop cannot be seen.
Which blood is mine to claim,
when ethnicity calls from the past?

Visions of love from those who made me,
divulges I am all of these human faces.
Do those who challenge my mirror image not matter,
or does their spite disappear in the winds of time?

Ancestral eyes stare from sleepy mists of history;
one drop reflections of their descendant successor.
Am I a one drop invisible Black person,
or a so-called mixed-race Delaware Moor?

July 1, 2018

Elizabeth Miller Parrish near the end of her life (ca. 1937).

Incognito

My Delaware Moor mother struggled to give me birth, which is why I exist
And so I love her and each grandmother, as far back as I can reach
That I might be who I am
That I might remember them as I do

I am the storyteller of my tribe, a chosen one
Those who have gone before, cry out to be remembered
I have been called to tell their story
In telling their story, I somehow find myself.

Light-skinned free persons of color
Imposters of invisible darkness
Who are mirrors of my soul
In the dusty mists of past brotherhoods and sisterhoods

Hidden identities concealed in my genes
An unknown surprise irony found
My mixed-blood crying out for illumination
Makes me a concealed chameleon

Distant warrior ancestors appear to me
Blending into the racial landscape of history
Knowing they sought survival from evil men
Their reasons for passing produces no shame

Discovery of being Black, thinking you are White
Is a dawn of freedom, crossing that color line
No fault found, for there are no lies when you do not know
Unveiling the shrouded mystery is a triumph of spirit

Long lived in forgotten shadows of ancestral fires
Eluding family origins purpose the salvation of my demise
Prior secret lives erased the truth of where I came from
But now realized, awakens me to the possibility of who I am

February 20, 2019

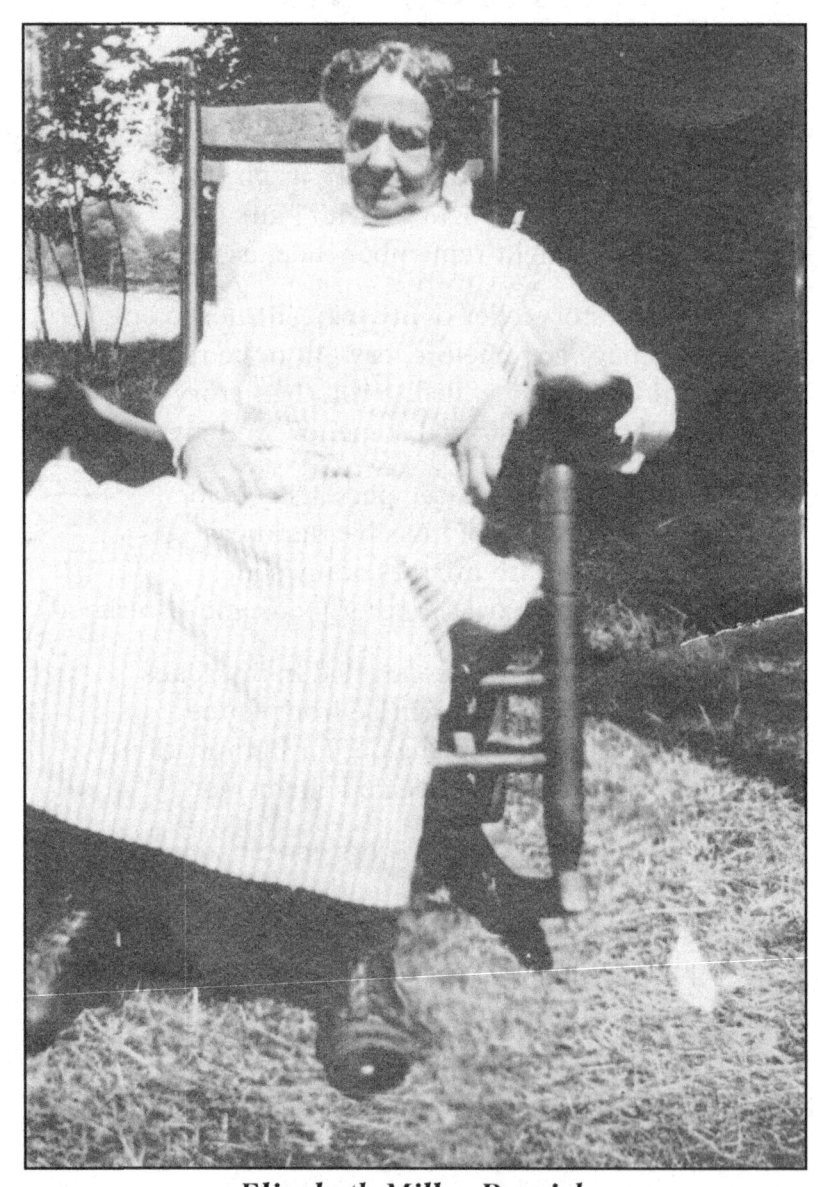

Elizabeth Miller Parrish
(My Delaware Moor great-grandmother).

Shine On

Forbears shine through the dimness of past midnights
As they shine, they become their own light in my world
Let them shine from past to present
May they continue to shine on all my tomorrows

My mixed-race ancestors shine like the stars and moon
Shine on forever as the rays of bright sunlight
Making their progeny smile in a rainbow of color
And keep on shining in the Black night or the White daylight

Dearly departed vital forces shine brightly
From dim darkness to dazzling brilliance
Their essence illuminates their descendant's duskiness
From dusk until dawn throughout history's hours of darkness

When the sunshine at night is gone I cannot see
Time gone by becomes shadows within the light
When past lives are kept secret causing great regret
Come into the light and expose the truth of who they are

Bygone family mysteries create a clandestine lie
Shine the light on these behind-the-scenes backstairs of deceit
Hush hush sneakiness betrays our isolated lineage
Who we are must be brought out into the light for all to see

Masked relatives are bloodlines not disclosed
The slow reveal shocks the uninformed
Such betrayal of human kind is a breach of trust
To expose what is behind the veil is to shine on

February 22, 2019

Elnora Parrish Williams in her 80s and her daughter, Vivian Williams Kelly Honea. The photo was taken in the front yard of Grandma's house in Stanton, Michigan, in 1968, the summer before Grandma passed.

Belonging

Racial mixtures provide no sense of belonging
Outwardly and inwardly not blending with their people
Interracial interactions brings forth multiple identity mindsets.
Turning away from both Blackness and Whiteness

Mixed, remixed heritage speakers
Ask am I really authentic?
Setting themselves up as judges
Of who is darkest Black or off-White

Beige rage insults the Blackish servant
Dusky hues of color create a master's rule
The whitest Black people dominate
As a river to their people.

The antagonists of mixed-heritage
Suffer no illusions of unity
They treat all hybrids with disrespect
And are transparent fanatics

Part of something more than themselves
Ancestors fleeing from South to North
Outsiders acting like something they are not
But perhaps something that they should be

A multi-racial actor not knowing where I belong
My familial past I want to know
My surprising present I wish to hold onto
My future belongs to this old soul, seeking my legacy

February 20, 2019

Grandpa Lewis Williams, sitting with his granddaughter Shirley Williams, and his son Tom Williams on the front lawn of his house in Stanton, Michigan, 1939.

My Delaware Moor Grandparents, Elnora Parrish Williams and Lewis Milton Williams, sitting in front of their house in Stanton, Michigan, in the late 1950s

Who We Be

Shadows of a racial Frankenstein; birthed into sinful slavery
Our ancestors, like mixed-blood caged animals
Chained in a bizarre menagerie of oppression and despair
Trapped in a painful void of bondage and collapse

Ethnic Samaritans traveling down that long Jericho Road
A perilous journey through the crossroads of fear and captivity towards freedom
Falling away from our Southern Blackness, into our Northern Whiteness
In the distant Michigan North Country, where our past did not matter.

My blended family navigating the Nanticoke River
Saving our Black souls by fleeing to the North and "passing"
Struggling with our transformation as invisible Black people
Paying the ultimate price of crossing over

A White painting in silhouette of a new life creation
Hidden profiles, once painted Black, White, and Indian
Now reimagined as a different color in-between the "color line"
Disguised for generations as a peerless pigmented impersonator

Racial brethren, throw off rebel shackles to be spiritually free, live a legacy that matters
Fooling the overpowering White ruling class for onehundred and fifty years
A parable of overcoming, amidst a former taskmaster, hiding behind a mantle of whiteness
Surviving citizen sons and daughters, who have lost our African and Native American culture

Who we be?
Isolated Delaware Moors christened as "Free Persons of Color"
Chosen out of slavery as "Free Blacks" and "Mulattos"
A metamorphosis of "free jacks;" passing as White, circumventing "Jim Crow"

September 17, 2019

Phoebe Carney (Libby) Miller
(My maternal Delaware Moor great-great-grandmother).

I Never Knew

My people never told me of my real ancestral home;
Those that came before sought to protect their own.
I never knew the old ones and who my ancestors were;
I never knew their sacrifice or what they had to endure.
I never knew about the family secret and why my mother cried;
I never knew until all of the old folks had died.

I never knew until I found out for myself, without any shame;
That what I am inside is to be loved and that no one is to blame.
I never knew who I truly was; hidden way down deep inside;
I do know now that I must tell it to all with great pride.
I never knew that I, child of my mother, was of mixed race;
Delaware Moor; the Yellow People; this is my true human face.

I never knew that I was White, Black, and Indian;
I never knew because others considered it to be an ultimate sin.
I never knew what my grandmother taught me came from Indian ways;
But loving memories of the touch of grandma's hands stays and stays.
It doesn't matter that I never knew;
It only matters that now I do.

August 27, 2006

Loren Kelly with his cousin Nancy Williams, playing on the dirt lane to Grandma Williams house, 1960.

Lewis Milton Williams with his grandson five-year-old Loren Kelly at the Williams House dump, Stanton, Michigan, 1956

Epilogue

I have always been an old soul. Sometimes I felt as if I were born in the wrong era of history and better suited for another century. As I have grown older, I began to realize if I did not write my family history someone else would. Because I am a historian and a genealogist, I believed someone else would dilute our story and not be as accurate, making me more determined to transcribe this family's story. I remember Mom telling me, when I was much younger, that our family was "Black Dutch," but I was too young to realize what that meant. I thought she meant we were part Dutch. Unbeknown to me at the time, she had pulled back the curtain and given me a peek at our family secret. "Black Dutch," was the term passed down through Southeastern U.S. families of mixed-race ancestry like my ancestors the Delaware Moors.

Sixteen years ago when I was fifty-three, I discovered I was multi-racial. Now I am sixty-nine, approaching the twilight of life and looking back on the early years. Time has given me a better understanding of my family. People are complicated and genealogy helps to flesh out personalities and the reasons behind decisions made through a lifetime. I have learned a noble act does not necessarily create a righteous person and an egregious act does not automatically spawn a terrible person. My research began with a curiosity about my mom's side of the family and why they passed as White. With fewer family members left to tell their stories, time was of the essence. I wanted to develop a clearer understanding of my lineage to pass down to my children and my children's children. To me that was a significant enough reason to follow the trail of my family roots and begin a journey of discovery. My mission on this ancestor hunt was to bring my people out of the shadows of history. It is important for me to share this commentary of who I really am.

By authoring this book, I sought to piece together memories of my mother's family with genealogical research. As I put the historical puzzle together, I began to rebuild my life—a life inextricably bound up with that of my mother and our ancestors. This chronicle consisted of memories my family created from their own experiences, passed down through oral and written history. While conducting my research, my thoughts alternated, between my races—first as Black, next as Native American, and finally as White. Ultimately, by the end of my introspective journey, I was able to claim all three races within me. I fully accept and identify my tri-racial identity. My mother adapted to her world and accepted her mixed-race through a personal negotiation of both her past and present. I have done the same through these mixed-blood stories, family images, and poetry. I am proud of who I am, because of where I come from.

This literary work constitutes historical memories from the past, enabling my ancestor's voices to be heard. "Passing" as White gave my ancestors a fighting chance for freedom. Our family evaded racial hatred in the South and achieved better lives in the North by leaping from one racial identity into an altogether different one. By accepting exile, they left behind friends, family and community. Most certainly, they experienced a sense of loss, loneliness, and grief by relinquishing their kinfolk and previous lives. A price they were willing to pay to live undetected among Whites and survive the threat of human bondage. Not only did they cross the *Mason-Dixon Line,* they crossed the *color line,* forfeiting their Black birthright. I am sure they *crossed over* with a heavy conscience, knowing the penalties for passing were severe. They successfully lived this subterfuge for 150 years. My family's story was a dramatic saga of a daunting struggle by an oppressed people longing to be truly free.

My forebearers were a different race of kinfolk and considered themselves as such. Self-identifying as Delaware Moor they said:

"I'm not White!...I'm not Black!...I'm not Indian!...I'm Delaware Moor!"

No more family secrets. What I have written is a reminder of where I came from. Every generation is somewhat different, but we must never forget our origins.

> Family...
>
> They are me and I am them...
>
> That's it...
>
> That's what is most important...
>
> That's what life is all about...
>
> Love for "kith and kin."
>
> **No more blood secret. This is who I am.**

Loren G. Kelly
March 3, 2020

'Wade in the Water'

A Civil War slave song whose lyrics were used to access the Underground Railroad. My ancestral Delaware Moors were persecuted Free Blacks, who sometimes fled North with fugitive slaves on the Underground Railroad.

Wade in the water, wade in the water, children
Wade in the water,
God's gonna' trouble the water

Who's that young girl dressed in red
Wade in the water
Must be the children that Moses led
God's gonna' trouble the water

Wade in the water, wade in the water, children
Wade in the water,
God's gonna' trouble the water

Who's that young girl dressed in white
Wade in the water
Must be the children of the Israelite
Oh, God's gonna' trouble the water

Wade in the water, wade in the water, children
Wade in the water,
God's gonna' trouble the water

Who's that young girl dressed in blue
Wade in the water
Must be the children that's coming through,
God's gonna' trouble the water, yeah

Wade in the water, wade in the water, children
Wade in the water,
God's gonna' trouble the water

You don't believe I've been redeemed,
Wade in the water
Just see the Holy Ghost looking for me
God's gonna' trouble the water

Wade in the water, wade in the water, children
Wade in the water,
God's gonna' trouble the water

*Songwriter(s) Unknown. First published in *New Jubilee Songs as Sung by the Fisk Jubilee Singers* (1901) by John Wesley Work II and his brother, Frederick J. Work.

Acknowledgements

Somewhere in the misty past is an ancestor whose emotional sensations and occasional imagery comes to me through a dream state or in a meditative moment. When I have this unusual feeling, the words begin to flow. This is my muse. Most writers understand this. I feel my muse is a spiritual ancestral connection, offering determined inspiration and a passionate voice of transcription. Incredibly, it is as if my lineage is speaking from the past. As a storyteller, this muse gives me the ability to paint a picture with words. I also believe our "Genes 'R' Us." I deduce the genetic memory of my ancestors survives through me. So I would like to thank all of my departed kinfolk, some of whom I have known in my lifetime and some of whom I have only met or will eventually meet in my meditative dream state of aesthetic writing.

I also wish to thank Grandma Elnora Parrish Williams who always believed in me and my abilities. Grandma was gifted and talented far beyond her grade school education. She had a passion for writing and telling stories. Grandma Williams played piano by ear and possessed an uncanny psychic ability. She bought my first harmonica for me, when I was nine years old, and still enjoy playing it. I seem to have inherited some of her talents. Grandma was a Christian woman who taught us about love of family. She was the only grandparent I ever really knew and I loved her dearly.

Of course I cannot give enough thanks to the woman who gave me life, my mother, Vivian Williams Kelly Honea. Especially when Mom sat down with me and identified the numerous photographs of our ancestors in her photo albums. Ma knew she was dying, so she gave all of them to me for safekeeping. She is the reason our family history will be preserved. I remembered the stories she so lovingly told about our family. Many of her stories and photographs are included in this book. Due to her unselfish efforts informing me about our family and what we represent, I was able to piece together this family narrative. I love and miss you, Mom.

And of course my eternal love and gratitude goes out to my sister, Lanora Kelly Owens, for allowing me to share her memories on these pages. She helped care for me when I was a little boy. Lanora would "teeter totter" with me in the park in our hometown of Phillips, Texas. She is my favorite and only sister. I wouldn't want another one. Lanora, I really enjoyed eating your red popsicles, when you took me to the park to play. As sister and brother, we had many conversations about family that played an important part in writing this book. I love you very much, Lanora.

Many thanks go out to my cousins, Shirley White, Nancy Schalk, Mark Forsberg, and Suzanne Krogman. Cousins are special relatives and these remaining grandchildren and great-grandchild of Elnora Parrish Williams are no exception. They allowed me to pick their brains about past family events. I could not have written this book without their memories of the fun times we had growing up. They loved Grandma Williams as much as my Mom, my sister, and I. I know they miss her. Amazingly, we are now the older generation of our Delaware Moor family and not many of us are left. I love all of you guys.

To my beautiful wife, Barbara Kelly, you are my friend, my one true love, and my soulmate. As we walk down this road of life together, please know I wouldn't want to take the journey with anyone else. Thank you for your loving support in our retirement years and standing by my side as I write these books about family. God has blessed us with a wonderful family and he has also blessed me with you.

A very special thanks to talented author, Millie Jean Coppedge, who recently passed. Millie was my original source of inspiration to become an author and will be sorely missed by everyone in our community. She once told me: "Loren, you have a way with words. You must write your book."

> *We never know how high we are*
> *Til we are called to rise;*
> *And then, if we are true to plan,*
> *Our statures touch the skies.*
> —Emily Dickinson

Millie, I know you have touched the skies and are now at peace.

And to my Editor, Vivian Freeman Chaffin of Yellow Rose Typesetting, thank you for all of your advice and hard work which has transformed me into a better writer.

I want to also thank my Lord and Savior, Jesus Christ, for giving me the gift to paint these pictures with words. All the honor and glory goes to God. In today's divided society, it would serve us all well to remember,

> "How good and pleasant it is when
> God's people live together in unity!"
> —Psalm 133:1

> "God's time is always near. He set the North Star in the heavens;
> He gave me the strength in my limbs; He meant I should be free."
> —Harriet Tubman
> (my eighth cousin, twice Removed)

We are the same; you and me. Set free by God, from our first breath, we are uncommon mortals. Destined to be individuals, but still the same. By inhaling the same air, we are as one. By bleeding the same blood, we bleed the same color red. We are human kindred souls, baptized together in our nation's melting pot. Enfolded in the patriotism of our Stars and Stripes, we are all Americans. We are the same—you and me.

—Loren G. Kelly
March 3, 2020

About the Author

Loren Kelly is a retired police officer and history teacher who lives in Royse City, Texas. Loren graduated from Phillips High School, Phillips, Texas, in 1969, subsequently attending Frank Phillips College, Borger, Texas, and graduating with an Associate of Arts with honors as a member of Phi Theta Kappa (The International Junior College Honor Society) in 1971. Loren then attended West Texas State University (now West Texas A&M University) in Canyon, Texas, earning a Bachelor of Science in History and a Secondary Social Studies Teacher's Certificate in 1974 and was also a member of Phi Alpha Theta (The International Honor Society of History). Loren retired from Dallas County, Texas, in 2016, following twenty-six years of service for a total of thirty-nine years in the field of Criminal Justice (1977-2016). As a former peace officer, Loren is a 1987 graduate of the Dallas County Sheriff's Department Police Academy. In 1981 he married his beautiful wife, Barbara Kelly. He and Barbara had four children and now have twelve grandchildren. Together they love to travel and have visited Ireland, England, France, Switzerland, Italy, Canada, and Hawaii since retirement. Loren is a Christian and an active member of the Community Baptist Church in Royse City, Texas. He is also a member of the Royse City Cultural Arts Committee that oversees the C. F. Goodwin Public Library and the Zaner Robison Historical Museum. Loren is a writer and avid reader/researcher of History as well as a genealogist who enjoys researching Family History.

Made in the USA
Coppell, TX
08 November 2024

39819930R10077